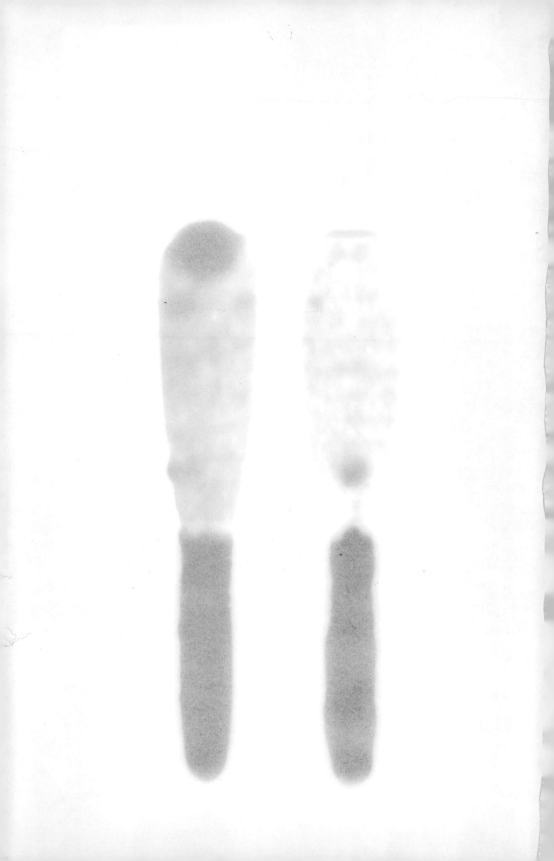

Capitalism and catastrophe

Capitalism and catastrophe

A critical appraisal of the limits to capitalism

STEPHEN ROUSSEAS

Vassar College

CAMBRIDGE UNIVERSITY PRESS

CAMBRIDGE
LONDON   NEW YORK   NEW ROCHELLE
MELBOURNE   SYDNEY

Published by the Press Syndicate of the University of Cambridge
The Pitt Building, Trumpington Street, Cambridge CB2 1RP
32 East 57th Street, New York, NY 10022, USA
296 Beaconsfield Parade, Middle Park, Melbourne 3206, Australia

First published 1979
Reprinted 1980

Printed in the United States of America
Typeset by The Composing Room of Michigan, Inc.,
Grand Rapids, Michigan
Printed and bound by The Book Press,
Brattleboro, Vermont

Library of Congress Cataloging in Publication Data

Rousseas, Stephen William.

Capitalism and catastrophe.

Includes bibliographical references.
1. Capitalism.   2. Marxian
economics.   I. Title.
HB501.R765   335.4'01   78-11996
ISBN 0 521 22333 4

To
Claude
and
Philip

Contents

Preface

This book is intended as a critical essay on the nature of advanced capitalism. Its origin was a paper written for a conference held at Rutgers University in April 1977 on "Post-Keynesian Theory: The Unexplored Issues." The conference was a gathering of economists who identify themselves with what has come to be known as the post-Keynesian revolt. Among the first to mount the barricades in the early sixties was Joan Robinson. Her attack on "pre-Keynesian economists *after* Keynes," to use her well-suited phrase, was devastating. She questioned not only the meaning of 'capital' in bastardized Keynesian theory, but also its use in a neoclassical theory of income distribution where the rewards of labor and capital are based on their relative contributions to the total output of goods and services under competitive market conditions. She accused them, in effect, of pushing the ideological bias of their neo-neo-classicism, namely, the ideology of the status quo, into the background while parading stage front in the pseudoscientific garments of a neutral, *wertfrei* economics. She was particularly severe on neoclassical equilibrium analysis and its use of static comparisons in logical time to analyze what is essentially a process taking place in historical time – where the past is opaquely dark, the future is unknown if not unknowable, and the present is the stomping ground of the intellectual mandarins.

The taming and the mechanical bowdlerization of the original Keynesian revolution had become a sore point with Joan Robinson, herself a contemporary of John Maynard Keynes and an influential contributor to his *General Theory*. While the 'New' Cambridge–New Haven axis reacted to the frontal attacks of Joan Robinson and other post-Keynesians by flooding the moats and lifting up the drawbridges of orthodoxy, the 'Old' Cambridge, on the other side of the Atlantic, undermined the neoclassical foundations by reviving an interest in the earlier theories of Ricardo and Marx and their concern over the class distribution of income.

In its simplest terms, the 'New' Cambridge neoclassicals see distribution as an aspect of pricing in a free market economy subject to the 'laws' of supply and demand. For Joan Robinson's 'Old' Cambridge, pricing is an aspect of distribution. Given the monopoly determination of prices, distribution is consequently a matter of *power* in a class society where the struggle over relative shares undermines the stability of the capitalist system. Because growth is the fundamental characteristic of capitalism, and because it is based on the profit expectations of capitalists, any serious attempt by labor to achieve a larger slice of the pie is bound to have an adverse effect on profits and thus on the viability of the system. In this schema, prices are determined by an historically set wage level, itself the result of the class struggle over relative shares. The theory of distribution therefore takes priority over an historically timeless theory of value operating in the vacuity of equilibrium analysis.

Building as she did on Ricardo, Marx, Michal Kalecki, and Pierro Sraffa, Robinson restored Keynesian theory to its original critical purpose and gave rise to what is now called post-Keynesian economics. She also tried, in the course of her work, to reformulate Marxian thought, but in her effort to demystify Marx she found that the fundamentalists put up a solid wall of resistance, as firm and as rocklike as that of 'bastard' Keynesians. Vulgar Marxism and vulgar Keynesianism clearly share one thing in common: a vulgarity based on scientific pretension and the 'discovery' of universal social 'laws'. With the exception of Robinson, however, most post-Keynesians have avoided excursions into the murky waters of Marxian theory; they have been too busy attacking the vulgar Keynesians on their own turf and from within the fold.

My concern in writing this book is that post-Keynesians, much as I agree with them, have neglected to review critically some fruitful neo-Marxian theories of advanced capitalism, particularly those of Jürgen Habermas and other members of the Frankfurt School of critical thought. It is this gap in their analysis that this book attempts to fill. In the process of trying to do so, I found it necessary to examine certain neo-Marxian theories on their own terms, just as the post-Keynesians did with their 'bastard' variety. I view my approach as complementary to post-Keynesian theory as it is evolving. My overall argument, though focused on the neo-Marxians, is in support of the post-Keynesian critique of vulgar Keynesianism *from another direction*, and it is for that reason alone that I have not presented a detailed exegesis of the post-Keynesian position.

In preparing the shorter paper for the Rutgers conference, I found myself forced to step back and look at Marxian theory itself and the schisms that were quick to appear after the death of Engels in 1895. The towering figure who emerges from these unseemly squabbles is

Rosa Luxemburg, and I pay especial attention to her catastrophe theory of capitalism. Catastrophe theories have never been popular in Marxist circles, at least not the one propounded by Luxemburg. Indeed, her magnum opus, *The Accumulation of Capital* (1913), has been rightly described by her biographer, Peter Nettl, as her *livre maudit*.

Luxemburg was a tempestuous and enigmatic woman. She could scale the heights of revolutionary ecstasy, only to plunge the next moment into the blackest despair. She could hate publicly with passion but love secretly and exclusively, demanding and giving all. Yet it was with cold precision that she abruptly ended a life's love because of a two-week dalliance of her lover, Leo Jogiches. She was neither forgiving nor tolerant by nature. She could dismiss individuals with scorn and contempt with no regard for their bruised egos. She judged people by her cat's initial reaction to them – a test that Lenin passed, apparently the only lapse in Mimi's otherwise infallible record. She was a woman of many paradoxes, who could hate the bourgeoisie while living like one of them (a true *gauchiste de luxe*); who could hate the Germans and yet die fighting for them. These are the paradoxes of a strange, intense woman possessed of a fiery but abrasive intelligence. A contentious, argumentative, self-assured woman, she was also a supreme journalist and pamphleteer who could, in more relaxed times, when she was the periodic "guest of the government," devote herself to botany, birds, and linguistics in prison and say that what she was really meant to do was tend the geese. She was an internationalist internationally famous at a time when Lenin was a factious and obscure revolutionary narrowly obsessed with Russia, who might well have remained obscure but for the success of the October Revolution.

Above all, Luxemburg was 'anti-systems', in that she distrusted any theory that claimed to have all the answers. She never balked at 'correcting' Marx, to the consternation of such older guardians of the Holy Writ as Plekhanov and Kautsky. Indeed, in *The Accumulation of Capital* she had the temerity both to say out loud that the posthumously published Volumes II and III of *Capital* were a mess and to offer a more coherent theory of capital accumulation. After the storm of her book subsided and after her brutal murder in 1919, she was relegated to oblivion by the rise of Leninist-Marxism (to put the matter in its correct reverse order), which culminated in the *Diamat* of Stalin. *Luxemburgism* became a very dirty word in 'official' Marxist circles and it is only recently that Western scholars have become interested in her work. Catastrophe theories are rather much in vogue once again, the Club of Rome being a recent example of this genus. The attacks on the Club of Rome from the economics establishment have been no less ferocious than the attacks by Marxists on Luxemburg's *The Accumulation of Capital* – though I would hardly equate the two. On the contrary, I would regard the Club of Rome as a rather dangerous development in advanced capitalist society, as I will argue later in this book.

My basic thesis is that Marxian theorists, both old and new, have underestimated the resiliency of capitalism and its remarkable instinct for survival. I have always felt that Marxists, while arguing over the timetable of capitalism's demise, have been too intent on exposing its 'internal contradictions' to view it as anything other than a "unity of contradictions," to use Bukharin's phrase. It is not a matter of whether or not one 'likes' capitalism. But if one does not like it, it is far more dangerous to underestimate its strengths than to overestimate its 'inherent' weaknesses. Even if capital accumulation has once again become the problematic of modern advanced capitalism, for largely *external* reasons, I do not expect it to collapse because of it. But even if it did I would seriously doubt, short of an atomic war, its inability to bounce back with the problem somewhat under control. As Alexander Herzen, the father of Russian populism, observed a long time ago, "The bourgeois world, blown up by gunpowder, will when the smoke settles and the ruins are cleared, arise again, with some modifications, as another sort of bourgeois world, because it is not yet internally exhausted and the new world is not ready to replace it."

It is this "other sort of bourgeois world" that I am concerned with, along with certain current developments that allow us to peek, however tentatively, into its possible paths of future development. I do not believe that the future can be predicted, the hubris of contemporary social science notwithstanding. But I do think we can delineate the 'field of possibles', to use an existentialist phrase, and make our commitments accordingly. Human history is, after all, for better or for worse, the sum of human commitments taken, consciously or not, within the constraints of a concrete historical existence.

Although I am not a Marxist, in the strict sense of that word, neither am I an anti-Marxist. Nor do I claim any expertise in Marxian theory. Having been raised in the pseudoscientific sterility of orthodox economics, with its penchant for problem solving without in any substantive way challenging or critically evaluating the status quo, the Marxian and neo-Marxian critiques of the capitalist system I can only view as a refreshing breeze in an otherwise stultifying atmosphere. But just as 'bourgeois' economists for too long have turned a deaf ear to Marxian theory, so have Marxists confined themselves to their own internal doctrinal disputes while dismissing non-Marxian economics as irrelevant rubbish.

To complicate matters further, all too many Marxists have a tendency to reserve for themselves the right to pass on the credentials of other Marxists and to drum out of the club anyone who dares to tamper with the basic doctrines of the Master. This, in fact, was the fate of Rosa Luxemburg. "Official 'experts' of Marxism," she argued in her *Anti-Critique* (1915), "violently attack anyone who thinks he sees a problem" in Marx's writings. To her this was a case of "blatant 'epigonism'." The "official custodians of Marxism," she wrote, "the 'supreme court' of 'experts' . . . give reports on whether or not people have understood or misunderstood the 'nature', aim and significance of Marx's models." This often fatal disease of Marxian scholarship goes under the name of *tsitatnichestvo,* or the use of numberless citations in lieu of expressed thoughts. An early symptom is a blinding faith in the infinite power of quotation, followed by an obsession for imposing a logical order upon the writings of Marx that in most instances is simply not there. The end result is the rigor mortis of an 'enforced schematism'. It was this benighted form of dogmatic Marxism that stuck in Luxemburg's craw. She concluded in *Anti-Critique:*

> Marxism is a revolutionary world outlook which must always strive for new discoveries, which completely despises rigidity in once-valid theses, and whose living force is best preserved in the intellectual clash of self-criticism and the rough and tumble of history.

It is in this spirit that this book has been written in response to those more-enlightened Marxists who, like Luxemburg, have tried to drag Marxism into the twentieth century in a more relevant and less dogmatic way. If I have been critical of some of them, it is not without admiration and respect for what they are trying to do: to find a way out of the current impasse and descent into barbarism, as they see it.

I would like to express my gratitude to Joan Robinson, Sidney Weintraub, and Alfred Eichner, who were kind enough to offer extensive written comments on the first draft. I am also indebted to Howard Ross for his patient reading of the manuscript while on vacation in France and for providing me with the title of the book. John Neumaier and my colleagues at Vassar College, William Lunt, Kenneth Koford, and David Schalk, were also generous with their time and suggestions.

Cap Ferret   STEPHEN ROUSSEAS

PART I

Marxian theories
of advanced capitalism

1

Science, technology, and Marx

I

Beginning on a note of fancy, suppose you were born in Europe 100 years ago, in 1877, and subsequently moved in the radical circles of your time. *Das Kapital* would have been published 10 years earlier and would have sold only 1,000 copies by the time of your birth. Marx and Engels would still be alive. And the 1848 revolutions would still be in peoples' minds, having occurred 29 years earlier. As you grew up, you would no doubt have heard of them, despairingly, from those who had directly experienced and survived the triumph of the bourgeoisie. The slaughter of the 1871 Paris Commune, having taken place only 6 years before your birth, would have been, during your youth, a vivid topic of conversation and recrimination in all radical circles – Marxian and anarchist.

Although you would have been six years old when Marx died, and eighteen at the death of Engels, good old Wilhelm Liebknecht would be around to tell you, at first hand, what Marx and Engels were *really* like. And floating in the air would be the competing ideas of Proudhon, Blanqui, Fourier, Lassalle – and Bakunin, who would be handing out membership cards freely to imaginary revolutionary societies with the sinister Nechaev lurking in the shadows.

During all this time, capitalism would have been growing by leaps and bounds, simultaneously providing, for the convinced, evidence of the prophetic genius of Marx and grist for the disemboweling revisionism of Eduard Bernstein. You might possibly have been embroiled in the controversies surrounding Rosa Luxemburg, Kautsky, and Plekhanov. And you would have witnessed, after the petulant destruction of the First International by Marx and Engels, its replacement by the Second International under the domination and control of August Bebel's *Sozialdemokratische Partei Deutschlands* (SPD). Like Marx himself in his lifetime, despite the tragic failures of 1848 and 1871, you would have been breathlessly awaiting the momentary outbreak of *the* revolution. Franz Mehring's "long wind of history"

3

would have long been replaced by the *bated breath of history*, with its promise of a more immediate salvation – one to be experienced in your own lifetime. Indeed, the very hope and meaning of your existence would have been predicated on that expectation.

Plekhanov and Lenin, during your early youth, would be in Geneva (before their own break), quarreling with and plotting against all the other Russians. By the turn of the century, the SPD would have grown enormously in size and international influence, with Kautsky grinding out instant Marxian interpretations to order and to fit whatever was afoot, promulgating at the same time new versions of the *minimum* and the *maximum* programs, with greater emphasis on the former because the latter would come in due course and of its own accord. At the same time, you would have been deafened by the din of the revolutionary Poles fighting over the 'National Question', while Leo Jogiches slinked about organizing everything in sight *sub rosa*.

As a contemporary and perhaps sympathetic ally of a very opinionated but brilliant Rosa Luxemburg, you would have contracted the revolutionary bug, calling for Bernstein's head as a first order of business, with the *minimalist* southern labor-union wing of the SPD calling for yours and, even more stridently, for hers. Despite all your efforts, the deep sleep of mud-and-blood activism would have arrived via Kautsky's mechanical Marxism requiring no praxis – your protestations notwithstanding that only a *maximalist* revolutionary activism, based on the creative spontaneity of the proletariat, could bring about the liberation of the masses.

In the meantime, Lenin, following his own maximalist line, would be forging his deadly concept of the Revolutionary Vanguard, linked more directly to the ideas of two earlier Russians, Nechaev and Tkachev, than to the very German Marx. Suddenly, at the age of thirty-seven, the butchery and nationalism of World War I would have doomed the Second International to an internecine war of its own and its ultimate extinction as a unifying international force for world socialism. And in the postwar German uprising of 1919 you, along with other prominent Spartakists, would have been brutally murdered, with the passive collaboration of the Social Democrats then in political power, and dumped into a muddy canal and left there to rot for four and a half months. But Lenin, with the help of Imperial Germany two years earlier, would have survived to lay the foundations of a deformed revolution.

Those were heady times, and though the revolutionaries of Western Europe failed, once again, they were never without hope and a revolutionary élan. Had you lived to be sixty-two, however, you would have witnessed the Great Purge Trials of the 1930s, the Hitler–Stalin pact, and the outbreak of World War II. Yet, through all this turbulence and horror, capitalism emerged virtually intact and in a stronger position than ever before – with socialism's revolutionary fervor transformed into an unyielding despair. Had you lived to the ripe old age of eighty-seven, you would have read the radical tracts of the 1960s, which decried the disappearance of the proletariat – the co-opted, wing-clipped angels of revolt – while looking in desperation to the outcasts, the disenfranchised, and other elements of the lumpenproletariat, as well as to alienated middle-class students, as the last hope for revolution.

But you most probably would not have been around in the 1970s, when critical minds turned their attention to an analysis of *advanced* capitalism, with all the old questions still setting the tone for lively conversations and debates. Will capitalism continue to be a viable system? Will it last? Or is it still doomed by its own internal contradictions, only of a kind now needing a larger time span to bring capitalism to its ultimate demise? Above all, *how has capitalism changed and in what directions, and what are the implications of those changes for Marxian theory and the future?*

For some contemporary radicals, the future is a matter of despair. They see the success of capitalism in its elasticity, its almost infinite ability to adapt to changing circumstances along lines that assure its continued existence. They see its greatest counterrevolutionary weapon as the very basis of its inner dynamic – *the ability of capitalism to accumulate capital without apparent limit and to realize a legitimating growth rate sufficient to absorb the proletariat with higher and higher levels of affluence, thus guaranteeing capitalism's continued existence unchallenged.*[1]

The despair engendered by the last 100 years has led to an appallingly low level of criticism in the United States, with neo-seminar-Marxists still scratching around in the well-tilled fields of 'internal contradictions' to plant their hopes in. In Cambridge, England, a brilliant attack was launched against the American vulgarization of Keynes. Instead of being welcomed as much-needed allies, the Cantabrigians were themselves attacked by the hard-core Left, on both sides of the Atlantic, for being pseudo-Marxists. Yet far more serious work is being done in France and Germany, where the main intellectual currents are running. The development of existential Marxism in France is a case in point, but beyond the scope of this book.[2] More attention will be paid to Germany and the 'critical theory' approach of Horkheimer and Adorno as extended and refined in the works of Jürgen Habermas and others of the Frankfurt School.

II

In an essay written in honor of Herbert Marcuse's seventieth birthday,[3] Habermas laid the foundations of his theory of advanced capitalism, which he then elaborated in his book, *Legitimation Crisis*.[4] Habermas states that we live in a world in which political domination, for the most part and for most people, is unacknowledged, with the social framework divorced from "reflection and rational reconstruction." The key to advanced capitalism is to be found in a *rationalization* that institutionalizes "a form of domination whose political character becomes unrecognizable."[5] This rationalization of the existing conditions of life is the end result of what he calls "purposive-rational action," a type of action that *legitimates* the power of advanced capitalism, thereby enabling it to control and dominate society.

The domination of society, however, depends on "the capacity and drive to maintain and extend the apparatus as a whole,"[6] which, in turn, is based on the domination of nature through capital accumulation and technology. It has not been an easy process. In the words of Nikolai Bukharin, "It has taken man centuries of bitter struggle to place his iron bit in nature's mouth." It is this bridling of nature, under capitalism, that has provided it with the wherewithal to co-opt the proletariat. Increases in productivity allow for higher standards of living and the legitimation of advanced capitalism. But it is not domination through technology but domination *as* technology – meaning the *social* organization of a technologically based order of production – that leads, ultimately, to a rationally authoritarian society.

As William Leiss has pointed out, it is nonsense to talk of dominating nature in a world of class divisions and antagonisms, where the appropriation of nature comes in the form of private property. In the absence of a classless society, in short, the domination of nature is simply another name for the domination of man.[7] Indeed, as Husserl argued, to the extent that science coupled with ideology extends its mastery over nature, it extends at the same time its mastery over mankind. It is this view of the "world as prey" (Horkheimer) that leads to the apparently limitless drive to accumulate capital in an unending progression of growth. But if the domination of nature leads, in a capitalist society, to the domination of man via the appropriation of nature in the form of private property (a theme, as we shall see, much emphasized by Marx in his 1844 *Paris Manuscripts*), it also has built into it the potential for increasing social conflict (which Rosa Luxemburg extended to the international sphere in her *Accumulation of Capital*). And it is here that Habermas's concept of purposive-rational action comes in. Its goal is the legitimation of the system through the application of scientific knowledge. Its purpose is not to order society rationally but to develop *crisis-avoidance* scenarios in the context of an incessant drive to accumulate capital. The purpose of advanced capitalism, therefore, is not to come to terms with or inter-act with nature but to dominate it as a means for dominating man. But as I will argue below, both the 'scientific' socialist versions of Marxism, as they are practiced today in Eastern Europe and the Soviet Union, and the purely theoretical post-Marxian formulations of Michael Tugan-Baranovsky and Luxemburg are indistinguishable from capitalism on this point and posit an even greater accumulation of capital than capitalism ever dreamed of. The end result could well be a more violent Marxian transgression of the limits of nature and a more rapid approach than capitalism to the ultimate disaster awaiting any economic system predicated on unlimited growth in its final con-frontation with nature in a finite economic universe.

In Habermas's analysis, at any rate, the capitalist mode of produc-tion is based on long-term continuous growth as "the self-propelling mechanism" of the economic system. It blindly seeks to break all bounds and limits as it smashes through to the infinite, with technological change serving as the dynamic driving force of the sys-tem. All supply curves, at least in the early stages of 'liberal' capitalism, appear to be infinitely elastic, with no apparent limit to capital ac-cumulation. "Capitalism," writes Habermas,[8] "is the *first* mode of production in world history to institutionalize self-sustaining growth."*

It was not until late in the nineteenth century that science and technology became interdependent, according to Habermas. Until that time, science "did not contribute to the acceleration of technical development." With the "growing interdependence of research and technology" in modern times, we have witnessed the conversion of science into *"the leading productive force"* upon which economic growth itself depends. With the "loyalty of the wage-earning masses" co-opted through an ever-growing reward structure, class antagonisms become latent.[9] As long as growth based on limitless capital accumula-tion is possible, the problem of exploitation and the distribution of the social product ceases to be a political or class problem.

---

*Some contemporary economists are prepared to carry the argument to absurd lengths by stating that growth is an innate attribute of human nature. In his book *Two cheers for affluent society* [(New York, 1974), p. 91; italics supplied], the English economist Wilfred Beckerman writes that "[*H*]*uman nature* has not yet abandoned the goal of increases in goods and services that are enjoyed." Consequently, "only an altogether unparalleled optimism can lead one to believe that the vast mass of the population will voluntarily accept an abandonment of the goal of economic growth." It would simply be unnatural!

Along similar lines, although from a non-Marxist perspective, Peter Passell and Leonard Ross[10] argue that the middle class of advanced capitalist society has the political power to prevent a more equitable and needed redistribution of income, without which the continued existence of capitalism is in doubt. Growth therefore is a necessary substitute for redistribution in order to maintain, in Habermasian terms, the legitimation of advanced capitalism. By making redistribution a political nonissue, growth promotes the stability of capitalist society by preventing a rise in the revolutionary consciousness of the wage-earning masses. Unlike Marxists, however, conventional economists like Passell and Ross do not view growth as an 'objective necessity' for capitalism but as a convenient and clever ploy for co-opting the masses in the name of social stability. Without growth, apparently, capitalism would collapse. It would seem, therefore, that Passell and Ross are closet Luxemburgists in that they have an implicit catastrophe theory of capitalism. If for some reason growth should *not* be possible, then capitalist society must collapse, albeit for political reasons and not out of logical necessity. Passell and Ross, however, were faced with a problem that seemed to unravel their theory of capitalist salvation through growth. Growth is usually associated with inflation (given the 'iron law' of the Phillips curve, which Passell and Ross uncritically accept) and inflation is generally thought to have negative redistribution effects. If this is so, then their theory vanishes into thin air, given the implacability of the middle class, and they are faced with the bleak prospect of catastrophe, growth or no growth. But Passell and Ross were not to be daunted by this little problem. They argued that inflation is a good thing because it redistributes income from the rich to the poor! The lengths to which some "economists" will go in order to maintain the integrity of a bad idea is a constant source of wonder.

To return to a more serious argument, the dethronement of Marx's labor theory of value follows, according to Habermas, from the emergence of technology as the leading productive force. Marxian theory, as a result, cannot be applied to advanced capitalist society as it stands; it needs to be adapted to the changed circumstances of capitalism. Labor, therefore, can no longer be considered an ontological category serving as the means by which man depasses his past and present. Science and technology have now become *the* leading productive force and an *independent* source of surplus value. "Capitalist society has changed," writes Habermas, "to the point where the two key categories of Marxian theory, namely, class struggle and ideology, *can no longer be employed as they stand.*"[11]

8

The hackles of any traditional Marxist are bound to be raised by this seemingly major overhaul of Marxian theory. The replacement of the labor theory of value with technology as the leading productive force, however, should not be taken as a matter to be resolved by empirical hypothesis testing. This has generally been a waste of time in the social sciences. Habermas's argument should be seen as an interpretive-explanatory approach that claims to be more fruitful in analyzing contemporary capitalism, and it is on this basis that his claim has merit. The labor theory of value was a useful device in the hands of Marx for explaining the phenomenon of exploitation, and for that purpose it did its job well. But to stick to it for *all* analytical purposes and under *all* historical conditions is to indulge in a 'fundamentalism' best left to the Bible belt and to Talmudic Marxists.[12]

Yet Habermas's argument is not new, nor is it a major revision of Marxian theory. Indeed, as we shall see in the next section, substantial traces of it can be found in Notebook VII of Marx's *Grundrisse*, written in February 1858, nine years before the publication of Volume I of *Capital*.[13]

III

Every society, whether it be capitalist or not, must meet two basic requirements. In the words of Rosa Luxemburg:

> *First,* it has to feed society, clothe it and satisfy cultural needs through material goods, i.e., it must produce the means of subsistence in the widest sense of the word for all classes and ages. *Secondly,* each form of production must replace used up raw materials, tools, factories and so on to allow the continued existence of society and the provision of work. *Without the satisfaction of these two major requirements of any human society, cultural development and progress would be impossible.*[14]

It remains to be added that the provision of the means of subsistence and the replacement of capital used up in the process of production depends on two basic inputs: *capital* and *labor*. Moreover, what distinguishes any given society from another is the *social relations* within which capital and labor are employed and combined. How these social relations are viewed, whether within them capital and labor are seen to be in a harmonious or antagonistic relationship, is what separates bourgeois from Marxian economics. The essential point, no matter which ideological camp one belongs to, is that there can be no capital without labor and no labor without capital. No human society, and especially a modern one, can function without both.

For Marx, the total social product of capital and labor is divided into constant capital, variable capital, and surplus value. Constant capital consists of circulating capital, which is totally consumed in the production process (raw materials and intermediate products), and that part of fixed capital (plant and equipment) used up in the same production time period. Constant capital therefore represents the money outlays for circulating capital and depreciation. The important thing for Marx, which distinguishes him from orthodox economists, is that constant capital of itself does not create value – this function is reserved exclusively for labor as *the* ontological category in Marx's system.

Because labor can never be abolished, even in a 'true' communist society, the essence of Man is to be found *at all times* in his labor and in his relation to material society. Yet, to say that labor is therefore an ontological category in Marx does not imply a 'positive' ontology in the empty, abstract sense of being outside history. At any particular moment, labor is historically situated and the 'facticity' of its existence is determined by the mode of production prevailing at that time. Under the 'facticity' of capitalism, for example, labor is alienated and estranged in Marx. Nevertheless, it contains within it the motive force of historical change. Labor is therefore a 'negative' ontological category, in that it is firmly rooted in the dialectic of history – but it *is* an ontological category, the interplay of 'essence' and 'facticity' notwithstanding.[15]

Another way of looking at labor is through Marx's concept of variable capital. Variable capital, in anticipation of future returns, is the wages bill paid by capitalists, or the monies they lay out in advance to purchase the labor power needed to produce the means of production and consumption that make up the total output in a year's time, for example. But it is only labor, according to the labor theory of value, that has the power to *create* value. All the components of constant capital merely represent a part of the real output of the labor time of earlier periods of production. They are the *congealed* labor of past expenditures of labor time used in the current production period – in combination with living labor and in proportions dictated by the given state of technology. Living labor, however, receives as wages the *minimum* socially required amount to keep body, soul, and the family together – in order to be able to replicate itself for future production time periods, for without labor not only would there be no output, there would be no capitalists as well.

Labor, in other words, gets only "what it has to have," no more, no less. Yet labor produces more value than it takes to maintain it. Total output therefore exceeds the wages bill. This overplus, or surplus value, accrues to the capitalists by virtue of their ownership of the means of production. In this sense, the rights of private property, sanctioned by the legal system and buttressed by the power of the state, are the cornerstone of the capitalist system. Or, in the words of Proudhon (who greatly influenced the thinking of the young Marx before he fell out of favor as a naive utopian socialist): *"All property is theft."* It robs the worker of a substantial part of the total value he alone produces.

The ultimate irony, assuming that workers consume all their income and therefore save nothing, is that the money outlays for variable capital return "down to the last penny, into the pockets of the capitalists . . . since it is the capitalists who sell the means of subsistence to the workers as commodities."[16] The capitalists, of course, feed themselves out of the surplus value they expropriate from the workers, but if in an all-out orgy they were to spend *all* their surplus value on champagne, caviar, fast cars, and palaces, then the economy would be no more than a "modernized slave system of medieval feudalism." There would be no accumulation of capital, no growth, and therefore no capitalist system as such. Admittedly, capitalists live well, but the force that drives them through their 'green fuse' is the realization of profits and the use of these profits to expand the capital base of their system further – in order to reap still greater amounts of surplus value to be used for still greater accumulations of capital and so on ad infinitum in upwardly ascending spirals of greater and greater exploitation.

The major problem for capitalism, however, is the *realization* of that portion of surplus value not consumed by capitalists (i.e., profits) in the form of new *net* additions to the stock of fixed capital, after allowing for replacement of depreciated capital. Whether this process of capital accumulation could go on forever and without limit became an issue that split the Marxist camp into opposing factions, with the competing epigones of Marx engaged in scathing, cannibalistic debates. The fact remains, independently of the debates, that the key to capitalism and its continued viability, in *any* Marxian context, rests solely on its ability to accumulate fixed capital; that is, machines. It is a small step, therefore, to see technology itself as the dynamic component of capitalism in its pursuit of ever-increasing amounts of surplus value via increasingly sophisticated equipment. Marx himself, especially in the *Grundrisse*, was not reluctant to take this step. "Nature builds no machines," he said. Machines are "products of human industry" that represent the imposition of "human will over nature, or of human participation in nature. They are *organs of the human brain, created by the human hand;* the power of knowledge objectified." Fixed capital, in short, indicates the degree to which "general social knowledge has become a *direct force of production*" (p. 706, Marx's italics).

With the development of capitalism, fixed capital looms larger on the horizon and in time overwhelms labor in the production process, with fixed capital no more than "the exchange of living labour for objectified labour" (p. 704). To an increasing extent, capital accumulation and the production of fixed capital as such (*not* the production of use values for purely consumption purposes) becomes the driving force behind capitalism. Production of the means of production emerges as the paramount activity or business of capitalism – although not without periodic crises. Marx was emphatic that as a creator of *wealth* fixed capital had become relatively independent of the labor time employed in creating it. Capital, in other words, had "conquered the production process as such" and in the process "direct labour and its quantity disappear as the determinant principle of production" (p. 700).

But there is more to the story than the mere substitution of capital for labor. In the process of accumulation, the very nature of fixed capital changes *qualitatively*. The production process itself is transformed from one of simple labor into "a *scientific process,* which subjugates the forces of nature and compels them to work in the service of human needs" (p. 700; italics supplied). It is here that science and technology enter into Marx's discussion in the *Grundrisse* of the capitalist mode of production. Technology becomes even more important than capital itself as the determinant force in the production process.

Indeed, Marx argues that the domination of nature through science and technology "works toward the *dissolution* [of capital itself] as the form dominating production" (p. 700; italics supplied). The "general social knowledge" that Marx talks about can be interpreted to mean that the technological applications of science serve as the mechanism through which the progressive supersedence of living labor by dead labor gives a *scientific* character to the production process. To dispel any doubts about this, Marx goes on to state: "As with the transformation of value into capital, so does it appear in the *further* development of capital that . . . *science too [is] among these productive forces*" (p. 699; italics supplied). The necessity of capital accumulation in a capitalist society, and the *realization* of capitalist profits in the form of fixed capital transformed by the discoveries of science, is simply another way of talking about capitalism's apparent and incurable addiction to economic growth as an end in itself. "[T]he greater the scale on which fixed capital develops," wrote Marx, ". . . the more does the *continuity of the production process* . . . become an externally compelling condition for the mode of production founded on capital" (p. 703; Marx's italics).

In Marx's view, "Those economists who, like Ricardo, conceived production as directly identical with the self-realization of capital – and hence were heedless to the barriers of consumption . . . – having in view only the development of the forces of production . . . – *supply without regard to demand* – have therefore grasped *the positive essence of capital* more correctly and deeply *than those who . . . emphasized the barriers of consumption . . .*" (p. 410; italics supplied). If Marx's concept of "consumption" were stretched to include investment demand, then in the long run it would appear that a lack of 'effective demand' is not the key to understanding the essence of the capitalist process "*[I]t is in the production of fixed capital that capital posits itself as an end-in-itself,*" argues Marx (p. 710; Marx's italics).

Much earlier in the *Grundrisse*, Marx addressed himself to the "contradiction between production and realization," that is, the problem of having aggregate demand equal to aggregate supply and whether there was any chronic tendency for supply to exceed demand, leading to a permanent crisis as the normal state of affairs in capitalist society. Marx was far from being a catastrophe theorist, as was Rosa Luxemburg. If there is a limit to growth, argued Marx, it is "not inherent to production generally, but to production founded on capital" (p. 415). As long as science and technology serve to realize capitalist profits in the form of more and more sophisticated fixed-capital equipment, however, there would appear to be no limit to capitalist growth *in the long run*.

Having sided with those who considered "supply without regard to demand" over those who emphasized "the barriers to consumption," Marx was dangerously flirting with the concept of Say's Law – that supply creates its own demand. But Marx never fully subscribed to Say's Law; he generally held it in contempt. He readily admitted that capitalism was subject to short-run periods of overproduction and underemployment, but they were not to be regarded as steps leading, in the long run, to a chronic state of overproduction with capitalism at the end of its tether. Nikolai Bukharin reinforced this view in saying that "a conflict between production and consumption, or what amounts to the same thing, a general over-production, is nothing other than a crisis." He denied most emphatically that "over-production must manifest itself *at all times* in a purely capitalist society."[17]

To put it in more explicit Marxian terminology, the demise of capitalism is not to be seen as a strictly *objective* necessity. The dialectic was a bit more convoluted. Crises of mounting severity would, in time, work on the subjective consciousness of the proletariat, thereby releasing the revolutionary potential of the proletariat, who alone would bring about the ultimate transcendence of the capitalist mode of production. On purely objective grounds, however, there was no crisis as such that the capitalists could not resolve in time, if time and the proletariat would only leave them alone. In Lukácsian terms, history could only reveal itself in the consciousness of the proletariat, and the sole purpose of capitalist crises was to awaken that consciousness. Without that awakening, capitalism could go on forever, crises or no crises. In short, unlimited capital accumulation, although it could *theoretically* go on forever, did not necessarily imply that capitalism would *in fact* go on forever. For a Marxist, that would be tantamount to displaying an appalling ignorance of the dialectic in history. The 'proof' that capitalist crises were not a permanent feature of capitalism lay, for orthodox Marxists, in the famous footnote in Marx's *Theories of Surplus Value*. In it Marx was contrasting Adam Smith's view on the falling rate of profit with Ricardo's counterargument that all capital can always be productively and profitably employed; that no matter how abundant capital might be, there was no reason for profits to fall unless for some reason wages rose due to an "increasing difficulty of providing food and necessaries for the increasing numbers of workmen." To this, Marx added the following statement:

> A distinction must be made here. When Adam Smith explains the fall in the rate of profit from an overabundance of capital, as an accumulation of capital, he is speaking of a *permanent* effect and this is wrong. As against this, the *transitory* over-abundance of capital, over-production and crises are something different. *Permanent crises do not exist.*[18]

However that might be (we shall return to this critical issue in the next chapter), in the *Grundrisse* the essence of Marx's argument was as follows (p. 701; italics supplied):

> Capital employs machinery . . . only to the extent that it enables the worker to work a larger part of his time for capital. . . . Through this process, the amount of labour necessary

for the production of a given object is indeed reduced to a minimum. . . . *Capital . . . – quite intentionally – reduces human labour, expenditure of energy, to a minimum.*

Capital, in other words, appropriates labor and absorbs it into itself – "as though its body were by love possessed" (Goethe, quoted by Marx). With the development of large industries and the concentration of capital in the hands of the few, science and technology become *the* major productive forces, for "Invention then becomes a business, and the application of science to direct production itself becomes a prospect which determines and solicits it" (p. 704). The net result is a "monstrous disproportion between the labour time applied, and its product . . . [forcing] the worker [to step] to the side of the production process instead of being its chief actor" (p. 705). Direct labor thus disappears "as the determinant principle of production . . . and is reduced . . . to a smaller proportion, . . . and [to a] subordinate moment, compared to general scientific labour, [the] technological application of natural sciences" (p. 700). Marx then goes on to drive the point home (p. 704; italics supplied):

> It is . . . the analysis and application of mechanical and chemical laws, arising directly out of science, which enables the machine [fixed capital] to perform the same labour as that previously performed by the worker. However, the development of machinery along this path occurs only when large industry has reached a higher stage [as in advanced capitalism], *and all the sciences have been pressed into the service of capital.* . . . Invention then becomes a business, and *the application of science to direct production becomes a prospect which determines and solicits it.*

And it is the division of labor, moreover, that allows the transformation of "workers' operations into more and more mechanical ones, so that at a certain point a mechanism can step into their places" (p. 704). Consequently, as capitalism becomes more advanced, "the creation of wealth comes to depend less on labour time" than on "the general state of science and the progress of technology, or the application of this science to production" (p. 704).

This certainly supports the first part of Habermas's argument that the growing interdependence of research and technology in advanced capitalism has converted science "into the leading productive force" in a system that is the first in human history to make a fetish out of economic growth and the endless capital accumulation required to sustain it. But what of the second part of Habermas's argument, that labor can no longer be considered an ontological category and that the labor theory of value must be dethroned? Although Marx never disowned the labor theory of value in any of his writings, he came closest to doing so in the *Grundrisse*. Having admitted the huge displacement of labor in the production process by capital, itself evolving qualitatively as a result of the technological innovations induced by scientific knowledge, Marx was forced to the following remarkable conclusion in the *Grundrisse* (p. 705; italics supplied):

> As soon as labour in the direct form has ceased to be the great well-spring of wealth, *labour time ceases and must cease to be its measure.*

It would be a very small step indeed from this to the total abandonment of the labor theory of value itself – which Tugan-Baranovsky and other Marxists did in fact take – and it would seem that in terms of Marx himself Habermas's major points are vindicated, though of course this does not settle the matter once and for all on that account alone. As for Habermas's claim that Marx's notions of class struggle and ideology must also be jettisoned, there can be no support for this position from Marx's own writings. However, historical events and the adaptive plasticity of capitalism certainly tend to support his claim, as later arguments will attempt to show – although Habermas continues to cling to the Marxian concept of capitalist 'internal contradictions', which will ultimately lead to its downfall. But before going into this, we should look at an earlier, and unknowing, incarnation of Marx's *Grundrisse* arguments and the thunder and lightning to which they gave rise. It should be kept in mind, however, that the protagonists involved could not possibly have had access to the *Grundrisse* and were therefore forced to restrict their arguments to Volume I of *Capital* and Marx's incomplete and often confused jottings that Engels put together as Volumes II and III.

2

The limit to capitalist growth

I

It would be boring to the point of pain were we to replicate Marx's simple and expanded capitalist reproduction schemata from Volume II of *Capital*.[1] Only a general outline will be given, along with the underlying assumptions of Marx's models, many of them implicit.

In Chapter XX of Volume II, Marx used a simple reproduction schema consisting of two Departments. Department I's output was restricted to the production of producers' goods (raw materials and fixed capital), and Department II specialized exclusively in the production of the means of subsistence (consumers' goods). Marx assumed that: (1) 'normal' prices prevail, that is, the market prices of goods reflect the amounts of labor value embodied in them, which in turn determine relative prices or rates of exchange embodying equivalent amounts of labor time, (2) real wages and real surplus value are constant on a per capita basis; (3) the stock of capital remains unchanged from one production time period to another, which implies that net investment is zero, meaning that there is no net addition to the existing stock of capital – gross investment in fixed capital is therefore equal to depreciation or the amount of wear and tear of the existing capital stock; and (4) the capital output ratio (c/o), the organic composition of capital (c/v), and the rate of surplus value (s/v) are the same for both Departments.

This highly abstract model was essentially static in that it illustrated the ex post facto equilibrium requirements of a closed economic system. The surplus output of producers' goods in Department I is just enough to replace the constant capital used up in Department II's production of consumers' goods. Or, to state the matter with its full implications, Department I exchanges its surplus production of producers' goods for an equivalent amount of Department II's consumers' goods surplus – which Department I needs for its physical survival. The remainder of each Department's output is consumed internally. In short, total output is exhausted, with the stock of capital main-

sumption was not critical to growth. "In a planned social production," wrote Tugan-Baranovsky, "if the leaders of production were equipped with all *information* about the demand and with the *power* to transfer labour and capital freely from one branch of production to another, then, however low the level of social consumption, *the supply of commodities would not exceed demand.*" [4] In a word: Say's Law. No less an authority than Rudolph Hilferding came down on Tugan-Baranovsky's side. "Any expansion of production" he argued, "is possible within the limit of existing productive forces ... [because] the outlet grows *automatically* with production."[5]

This did not rule out the possibility of crises if capitalists did not have all the "information" or the requisite will or "power" to shift labor and capital around, as needed for the establishment of a supply–demand equilibrium. In that eventuality, there would be a "lack of proportion," with an excess of aggregate supply over demand and a downturn in the economy as a result; and conversely in the case of excess demand. But the market under competitive conditions would quickly establish the needed proportions so that over the long run, when all the ups and downs cancel each other out, capitalism's natural course would be on an upward trend of higher and higher capital accumulation – without apparent limit. All this on the basis of Marx's expanded reproduction schema, adequately modified to reach the necessary conclusions, which Luxemburg dismissed contemptuously as a futile "arithmetical exercise on paper" with no bearing whatever on the actual state of affairs. But she did concede that Tugan-Baranovsky had one *indirect* proof for his, and we might add, Habermas's and Marx's *Grundrisse* theses. In the words of Tugan-Baranovsky:

> Technical progress is expressed by the fact that ... the machine increases more and more in importance as compared to living labor, to the worker himself. ... Compared to the machine, the worker recedes further into the background and the demand resulting from the consumption of the workers is also put into the shade by that which results from productive consumption by the means of production. *The entire workings of a capitalist economy take on the character of a mechanism on its own.*[6]

Not surprisingly, Tugan-Baranovsky anticipated the main element of Habermas's later argument and, according to Luxemburg, stated baldly that *"Marx was completely wrong ... in assuming that man alone, not the machine, too, can be the creator of surplus value."*[7] This went further than Marx's admission in the *Grundrisse* that the machine (especially under a technology that gives rise to increasingly sophisticated machines, presumably of the capital-using or labor-saving variety) has largely displaced labor as the creator of wealth. But the difference between the two positions is not all that great, particularly if one regards the labor theory of value merely as a metaphor or as a technical theoretical device for illuminating the idea of exploitation and that once this is done, capital can be given its due as the principal creator of value as well as of wealth. It is quite possible, moreover, to explain the exploitative nature of capitalism without basing it on the labor theory of value. Even contemporary neoclassical marginal productivity theory, which allows capital its due for its contribution to total output, can be used to illustrate the case of exploitation under conditions of pure competition. The nub of the matter is that it is the private ownership of the means of production under oligopolistic conditions of market power that leads to an inequitable distribution of income under capitalism. This was exactly Marx's argument in 1844. In the *Paris Manuscripts* he had not yet formulated his version of the labor theory of value. Instead, he emphasized private property as the basis for alienated or estranged labor, the link between the two being the main theme of the 1844 *Manuscripts*. The full-blown Marxian labor theory of value was a much later product. All the labor theory of value allows is a pseudoscientific or seemingly objective 'proof' of capitalist exploitation. It is not necessary, and the measurement problems associated with the labor theory of value and its derivative, the concept of surplus value, are too well known to be recounted.[8]

In any event, the entire theoretical structure of Tugan-Baranovsky's "faulty" system rested, according to Luxemburg, on the principle "that in a capitalist society human consumption becomes increasingly unimportant, and production more and more an end in itself." She tied Lenin to this thesis of "production as an end in itself"; that "the department of social production which creates producer goods" grows more and more rapidly than the department creating consumers' goods.[9] Had she known the *Grundrisse*, she could have hitched Marx, too, to that wagon. To Luxemburg it was a "howler" that Bulgakov, Lenin, and Tugan-Baranovsky thought that they had found the "essential nature" of capitalism as "an economic system in which production is an end in itself and human consumption merely incidental."[10]* She felt that they had not only overstated their case, they had done worse: They had proven the invincibility of capitalism!

---

*Nelson Rockefeller, however, would not have regarded it as a "howler": "I would think, generally speaking, that we have got to channel more of our gross national product into capital formation for investment in new production ... *with a smaller*

Two issues were involved: one having to do with the displacement of labor by capital, the other with the related acceleration of qualitative capital accumulation due to technological changes induced by the progress of scientific knowledge. It was Tugan-Baranovsky's unrestricted linking of the two that gave rise to Luxemburg's ire, for without a limit to capitalist accumulation, socialism was dead. An extended quotation from Luxemburg will serve to give the sharp flavor of her incredulity.

> These Marxists ... [have offered] theoretical proof that capitalism can go on forever. *Assuming the accumulation of capital to be without limits, one has obviously proved the unlimited capacity of capitalism to survive!* Accumulation is the specifically capitalist method ... of economic progress. If the capitalist mode of production can ensure boundless expansion ... it is invincible indeed. The most important objective argument in support of socialist theory breaks down; socialist political action and the ideological import of the proletarian class struggle cease to reflect economic events, and socialism no longer appears an historical necessity. *Setting out to show that capitalism is possible, this trend of reasoning ends up by showing that socialism is impossible.*[11]

As if the point were not clear enough, she goes on to say that "Tugan-Baranovsky ... with the crude joy of a barbarian destroys all objective economic arguments in support of socialism."[12] He and his cohorts were, in this respect, indistinguishable from bourgeois economists.

III

After the abortive Russian Revolution of 1905, Luxemburg was more of a pariah than ever. She had become a gadfly to the trade-union wing of the SPD, accusing its leaders of "economism" or the subordination of revolutionary political activity to the interests of the trade-union movement alone. And through her uncompromising espousal of mass action and mass strike, she had also alienated the leadership

percentage of GNP going to the consumer. ... It is essential that the country recognize our national interest and shape its tax structure and incentives in such a way as to result in accumulating the capital to put in [to production]. If they change the [oil] depletion allowance, then there has to be some other provision to permit the accumulation of capital." Quoted in the *New York Times,* December 15, 1974, when Rockefeller was chosen to serve as vice-president by President Ford; italics supplied.

of the SPD itself by accusing it of "parliamentarianism," especially after their sharp defeat in the Reichstag elections of 1906. Even her private life was in disarray, the long love affair with Leo Jogiches having come to an abrupt and painful end.

With her fortunes at so low an ebb, the Prussian police came inadvertently to her aid. The SPD in 1906 had set up its own Central Party School in Berlin, staffed with such luminaries as Franz Mehring, Heinrich Schultz, Rudolph Hilferding, and Bremen Pannekoek. The Prussian police, in an act of harassment, threatened the expulsion of Hilferding (an Austrian) and Pannekoek (a Dutchman) from Germany as foreigners, forcing them to withdraw from the school.[13] With the support of her friend, Clara Zetkin, a member of the school's Supervisory Board, Luxemburg managed to be appointed to the faculty in 1907. She was well qualified for the position, having received her doctorate in economics in 1897 at the University of Zurich upon completion of her dissertation, *The Industrial Development of Poland.*

Until the outbreak of World War I in 1914, when the school was forced to close down, Luxemburg taught political economy and economic history. Although she had always had a profound contempt for pettifogging academics, she made an excellent and popular teacher, and it was during her tenure at the Central Party School that she started work on a textbook, *Introduction to Political Economy,* based on her lectures.[14] It was in trying to explain Marxian theory to her students and in trying to write it up in a coherent and logical way that she became progressively aware of its profound contradictions. Her approach to Marx was as aberrant as were her radical political activities – from the point of view of the 'official guardians' of orthodoxy. As a Marxist, Luxemburg's approach to Marx was more critical than venerating. And it was in trying to resolve the problems she had come across in Marx's expanded reproduction schema in Volume II of *Capital* that she was led to write her great and controversial book, *The Accumulation of Capital,* published on the eve of the outbreak of war in 1913. The storm it provoked is unparalleled in the annals of Marxism.

The problem was that all Marx's reproduction schemata were ex post facto equilibrium models that showed where one would have to be to get to where one *wanted* to be. Luxemburg's approach was ex ante: *How* does one get to where one wants to be and what conditions must be satisfied in order to get there in the first place, if indeed one can get there at all? Or, to put the matter in another way, in static analysis we are *here* and not *there*. In comparative statics we are *there* and not at the here of before. But we don't know how we got from *here* to *there*, that is, we do not know the *dynamics* of going from one place to another. Luxemburg's objections were to the static pushing around of numbers, as she sarcastically observed, "on uncomplaining paper."[15]

Any realistic analysis of capitalism requires an explanation of its metabolism and the historical context of its evolution, matters that were not fully addressed in Marx's expanded reproduction schema. Moreover, Marx's model of simple reproduction and his model of capital accumulation and growth in Volume II assumed the exclusive and universal existence of a capitalist economy, thus ignoring the concrete historical realities of capitalism. In her *Anti-Critique*, which gives a far clearer exposition of her theory than *Accumulation*, she did not hesitate to quote the relevant passages from Marx.[16] In Volume I, Marx explained the basic premise of his methodological approach in a footnote:

> In order to examine the object of our investigation in its integrity, free from all disturbing circumstances, we must treat the whole world as one nation, and *assume that capitalist production is everywhere established and has possessed itself of every branch of industry.*

And in Volume II the same assumption was made in his development of expanded reproduction:

> Apart from [the capitalist] class, according to our assumption
> – *the general and exclusive domination of capitalist production* –
> there is no other class at all except the working class.

For Luxemburg, this was the root of the problem, for "In reality capitalist production is not the sole and completely dominating form of production" (*Anti-Critique*, p. 58). Marx's models were fine, in their simplified form, for analyzing individual capital and the phenomenon of capitalist exploitation, but given his assumption that "all other forms of economy and society have already disappeared," asked Luxemburg, "how can one explain imperialism in a society where there is no longer any space for it?" (p. 61). Marx's model was therefore inadequate to "deal with the accumulation of gross capital," because capital accumulation is an *historical* process that can only develop "in an environment of various pre-capitalist formations." The true nature of capital accumulation could not be captured in a "bloodless theoretical fiction," for "Marx himself only posed the question of the accumulation of gross capital, but his answer went no further" (pp. 61–2). She was quick to recognize that Volume II was an incomplete work, "only a torso, a loose collection of more or less finished fragments and drafts" (p. 63). For Luxemburg, "the problem of accumulation is itself purely economic and social: *it does not have anything to do with mathematical formulae"* (p. 48; italics supplied). The only thing Marx's models were capable of showing was "the proportion which, *if it is followed,* allows undisturbed accumulation" (p. 84; italics supplied). She had a firm grasp of the ex post facto limitations of Marx's models and she was equally aware that Marx had provided no explanation of *why* the equilibrium proportion should be reached or why anyone could expect this to be the long-run inner dynamic of capitalism, Marx's short-run periodic crises notwithstanding. Luxemburg moved into the void expecting hosannas but reaped brickbats instead.

IV

Luxemburg's critique began with Marx's static expanded reproduction schema and its total neglect of technological change. By introducing technological change into the model, the organic composition of capital (c/v) rises, as does the rate of surplus value. This, however, is based on a critical assumption in Luxemburg's analysis, namely, that real wages do not increase and are maintained at the socially determined minimum.[17] As a result, the full 'realization' of surplus value in new machines and equipment (fixed capital) would generate such an increase in the productive capacity of the economy that total output would far exceed the ability of Departments I and II to absorb it. What we would have, in modern parlance, is an excess of aggregate supply over demand or, equivalently, an insufficiency of effective demand. Or, to put the matter in still another way, there would be no reason and no incentive for capitalists to 'realize' all their surplus value (or, more accurately, that part not personally consumed by them) in the form of increased productive capacity if there were no assurance that the additional output of such net investment could be profitably sold. Therefore, in a universally closed capitalist system, according to Luxemburg, the insurmountable contradiction is between the production of surplus value and its 'realization', that is, between production (output) and its consumption. "Accumulation," argued Luxemburg, "cannot be confined to the mutual relations of purely capitalist industry" (p. 98). No matter what Tugan-Baranovsky, Hilferding, and other misguided Marxists thought, Say's Law did not apply.

Luxemburg's emphasis on effective demand contradicted head-on Tugan-Baranovsky's denial of the possibility of overproduction and provided her with the means for 'disproving' his thesis of unlimited capital accumulation. The problem of capitalism was not *crises* born of 'disproportionalities', but the imminent and inevitable *catastrophic col-*

lapse once capitalism evolved historically into a truly closed system in which capital accumulation would no longer be possible.[18]

Having 'proved' that capitalist accumulation, without which capitalism cannot survive, was impossible in a closed system, she had to explain why (in 1913) capitalism was indeed expanding. The answer was simple: Capitalism was still an open system. She appealed to "reality" (pp. 58–9):

> In reality, there are in all capitalist countries, even those with the most developed large-scale industry, numerous artisan and peasant enterprises which are engaged in simple commodity production. In reality, alongside the old capitalist countries there are still those even in Europe where peasant and artisan production is still strongly predominant.... And finally, there are huge continents besides capitalist Europe and North America, where capitalist production has only scattered roots, and apart from that the people of these continents have all sorts of economic systems.

The very viability of capitalism, given its absolute need to realize and capitalize surplus value in full, depends on these internal as well as external pockets of precapitalist production. As long as markets external to capitalism exist, as long, in other words, as capitalism exists in a world of capitalist *and* underdeveloped countries, capital can indeed be accumulated without apparent limit. But this is an illusion sustainable only in the short run. In the long run, as capitalism succeeds in transforming all the world into the capitalist mode of production, it will then be at the end of its tether, having transformed itself in the process into a *closed* system within which capital accumulation will no longer be possible. Much like contemporary limits-to-growth theories, catastrophe will ensue and capitalism, *theoretically,* will destroy itself in one fell swoop – though in reality its catastrophic demise will occur *before* the theoretical limit is reached.[19]

Luxemburg, in short, had reintroduced the notion of internal contradiction into the development of capitalist society: There was a limit to capital accumulation after all. The ultimate and universal aim of capitalism was clear in Luxemburg's mind. It was:

> ... to establish exclusive and universal domination of capitalist production in all countries and for all branches of industry.... As soon as this final result is achieved – *in theory, of course, because it can never actually happen* – accumulation must come to a stop. The realisation and capitalisation of surplus value become impossible to accomplish ... and

capitalist production is *in extremis*. For capital, the standstill of accumulation means that the development of productive forces is arrested, and the collapse of capitalism follows inevitably, as an *objective* historical necessity. *This is the reason for the contradictory behaviour of capitalism in the final stage of its historical career: imperialism.*[20]

Having denied the validity of Marx's original schema of expanded reproduction as being too static to explain the true nature of capitalist development, and having argued that capital accumulation "is more than an internal relationship; *it is primarily a relationship between capital and a non-capitalist environment,*"[21] Luxemburg had arrived at a full-fledged theory of imperialism. "There is no doubt," she wrote in her *Anti-Critique,* "that the explanation for the economic roots of imperialism must be deduced from the laws of capital accumulation . . . since imperialism as a whole is nothing but a specified method of accumulation" (p. 61). Imperialism was not to be seen merely as "a simple vice of the bourgeoisie" but as an "historical necessity," for capital accumulation, so vital to the existence and continued viability of capitalism, can only take place in an open system with *external* markets. This, to Luxemburg, "was the essential precondition for accumulation" – and for imperialism with its plunder and its incessant demand for new markets and outlets for its surplus output.[22]

Apart from her theory of imperialism, which is an appendage to her theory of capital accumulation, Luxemburg's main thesis was the absolute contradiction inherent in capitalist production and, consequently, the demise of capitalism as an 'objective' historical necessity. Her theory of capital accumulation came full circle, back to Marx's model of expanded reproduction and its assumption of the universal spread of capitalism. Luxemburg was fully aware of the one-whirl nature of her merry-go-round (pp. 145–6; italics supplied):

> Capital accumulation progresses and expands at the expense of non-capitalist strata and countries, squeezing them out at an ever faster rate. The general tendency and final result of this process is the exclusive world rule of capitalist production. *Once this is reached, Marx's model becomes valid:* accumulation, i.e., further expansion of capital, becomes impossible. *Capitalism comes to a dead end . . . it reaches its objective limit.*

The function of imperialism is to speed the process up, to accelerate capitalism's approach to its objective limit. But long before this *theoretical* limit is reached, the very process of imperialism functions in still another way: It prevents capitalism from reaching the objective limit in a series of "political and social catastrophes and convulsions" that, together with periodic economic crises, "make continued accumulation impossible and the rebellion of the international working class against the rule of capital necessary, *even before it has economically reached the limits it set for itself*" (p. 146; italics supplied).

Imperialism in its double function of impelling capitalism toward its theoretical limit and blowing it up before it gets there is, to Luxemburg, "only the last chapter of . . . [capitalism's] historical process of expansion" (p. 147). The series of catastrophes facing capitalism can have either of two outcomes: either "the decline of civilization *or* the transition to the socialist mode of production" (p. 147; italics supplied). The "or" of this quotation is critical and was to be repeated in her famous *Junius Pamphlet* (1916), in which she posed the question, "Barbarism *or* Socialism?" The use of "or" seemed to leave it an open question as to whether or not socialism would succeed capitalism as a matter of historical necessity. There seemed to be a contingency in history that precluded posing socialism's supersession of capitalism as an inevitable consequence of capitalism's historical development. Socialism could only be achieved through the conscious efforts of the proletariat, but no prior guaranty of success was possible.

Luxemburg's critics failed to understand the nuances of her use of the word 'objective' and its link to 'necessity'. They ignored her life-long emphasis on the 'Subject' and chose instead to accuse her of a mechanical fatalism; of an historical determinism that obviated the need for party organization or radical political activism; and of saying that all one had to do was to sit patiently on the historical sidelines, await the inevitable destruction of capitalism, and only then walk in, pick up the pieces, and reassemble them in socialist form. They deliberately overlooked her theory of spontaneity, her blistering attacks on the SPD for its passivity, and the grave doubts and depression to which she was always prone. It was a complete perversion of her life and works.

V

Luxemburg's theory of capitalist accumulation and imperialism (the subtitle of her book on capital accumulation being *A Contribution to the Economic Explanation of Imperialism*) outraged other Marxists, just as Tugan-Baranovsky and his followers had outraged her. One of her foremost critics, besides Otto Bauer, was none other than the biggest of all Marxist guns, Nikolai Bukharin himself. Although Luxemburg's *Accumulation* had been published in 1913 (and her *Anti-Critique,* posthumously, in 1921), Bukharin's attack in *Imperialism and the Accumula-*

tion of Capital did not come out until 1924, and then in simultaneous German and Russian editions.[23] Bukharin's anti-anti-critique was more respectful of Luxemburg as an intellectual and far less vituperative in its attack, but it was equally as total in its rejection of her main thesis as the other critics had been. In the main part of his attack, Bukharin employed a single-world capitalist trust to prove the viability of Marx's expanded reproduction model. In so doing, however, he obliterated Marx's basic notion of the anarchy of competitive capitalist production and fell into the trap of Say's Law in order to achieve a perpetual general equilbrium model that, although closed, permitted an endless process of capitalist accumulation. His technical attack, however, is far less interesting than the political motivation behind his critique.

Although Luxemburg had restored the basic Marxian concept of dialectical contradiction to capitalism, it wasn't good enough for Bukharin. The standard Marxist objections to Luxemburg's thesis are neatly summarized by the editor of the English edition of her *Anti-Critique* (pp. 31–2): (1) that Luxemburg "changed the basis of capitalist accumulation from something derived from surplus labour into a process which draws its main sustenance from an outside source"; (2) that "she . . . made the exploitation of the 'third' market the driving force of capitalism, not the exploitation of wage labour," which leads to the notion that surplus value is extracted from the 'third' market rather than from the indigenous working class; (3) that "the necessity of a proletariat revolution is no longer a valid proposition in the advanced capitalist countries," because the proletariat of these countries increase their real wages by becoming "joint exploiters with the capitalist class"; and, finally, (4) that the capitalists' local and co-opted proletariat would become politically passive and in the event of a 'third' world revolt "join with their respective capitalist class to beat back" the revolt.

Although touching on most of these points, Bukharin went beyond these perversions of Luxemburg's position. Writing in 1924, Bukharin was convinced that the successful Russian October Revolution had already illustrated and was evidence for the beginning of the end of capitalism, even though "three quarters of the world's population still remain in their capacity of 'third' persons." He announced: "The collapse of capitalism has started. The October Revolution is the most convincing living expression of that" (p. 266). This alone was sufficient to demonstrate the falseness of Luxemburg's theory. Moreover, "The *fact* of the existence of immense numbers of 'third persons' contradicts Rosa's theory of collapse," he proclaimed (p. 263; Bukharin's italics). But what really bothered Bukharin was the colorless "dullness" of her catastrophe theory. The 'third persons' could no longer be viewed "as potential allies of the proletariat in the class struggle" (p. 269), contrary to *Lenin's* views on the subject – another nail in Luxemburg's coffin!

The key to Bukharin's dissatisfaction, however, lay elsewhere. Apart from his concern that Luxemburg had shifted the emphasis of Marxian theory from the basic concept of 'exploitation' to the problem of 'realization',[24] he was in a greater hurry than Luxemburg (pp. 260–1, 263; italics supplied):

> Even if Rosa Luxemburg's theory were even approximately correct, the cause of revolution would be in a really poor position. For, given the existence of such a huge reservoir of 'third persons', ... there can be practically no talk of a collapse. ... [C]apitalist expansion [would still have] such a colossal field of activity at its disposal in the form of 'third persons', that only utopians [could] talk of some kind of proletarian revolution. The reality is that the illusion of an imminent victory of socialism [will have] collapsed. ... The reality [would be] that one [could] not yet anticipate the end of capitalist development. ... [Rosa's] conclusions *make revolution appear impossible for a long time.*

The bated breath of history once again! In effect, Luxemburg was guilty of the same crime she had indicted others for, only in her case the end, though possible, was much too far away to be acceptable. Bukharin's impatience aside, for Luxemburg a 'good' Marxist could not under any circumstance affirm that a limit to capitalist accumulation did not exist. If it did not, then socialism was doomed. Still, within Luxemburg's thesis, capitalist accumulation would be able to go on for a long, long time, as Bukharin pointed out, before it came even close to, let alone face to face with, her limiting *theoretical* wall of universal capitalism. Most probably, it was this realization that led to her theory of imperialism as a means of speeding up the process of destruction.* The holocaust of imperialist wars would appear well before the theoretical limit of capitalism were reached. Luxemburg envisioned "increasingly severe competition" among capitalist countries vying for control over the noncapitalist areas of the world. Imperialism works against itself: It extends the life of capitalism while at the same time shortening it. "The mere tendency towards imperialism," she wrote,

---

*Bukharin sensed this uncomfortableness in Luxemburg when he wrote (p. 261): "Rosa seems to be aware of the awkwardness of her whole proof. She admits that it would be ridiculous to assert that capitalism must first throttle every 'third person'. She explicitly states that capitalism will be blown up 'much earlier'."

"of itself takes forms *which make the final phase of capitalism a period of catastrophe.*"[25]

Bukharin's theory of imperialism, in a world where three-quarters of the population lived in precapitalist enclaves, was different. It was the drive for superprofits and access to raw materials that led to imperialism. It was not the inevitable consequence of the inability of capitalists to 'realize' their surplus value. As for the collapse of capitalism, it was not a mechanical inevitability but the result of what he called a "unity of contradictions," in which the dialectical unraveling of capitalism was a matter of a "continued reproduction of the capitalist contradiction" that would "blow up the entire capitalist system as a whole." But "how acute these contradictions have to become to blow up the system" he left an open question (p. 264). Bukharin did not deny the possibility of overproduction and an insufficiency of effective demand, but this was a matter of short-run periodic capitalist crises increasing in severity and ultimately triggering the revolt of the proletariat. He quoted Lenin to the effect that overproduction crises are inevitable in capitalist society, but the explanation for Lenin lay in "the *disturbance in proportion* between the various branches of industry" (quoted on p. 204; italics supplied), and not to a permanent *realization* problem, as in Luxemburg. To clinch the matter, Marx's footnote in his *Theories of Surplus Value* is repeatedly cited, as if this should settle the matter once and for all: "Permanent crises do not exist."

Bukharin linked Marx and Lenin to Tugan-Baranovsky and Hilferding in opposition to Luxemburg. Marx, Lenin, Tugan-Baranovsky, and Hilferding shared one common theoretical premise: "Crises stem from the disproportion between individual branches of production" (p. 225). Their difference, which was of lesser importance to Bukharin, lay over whether consumption was a "component part of this disproportionality," which of course Tugan-Baranovsky and Hilferding denied. At any rate, if Luxemburg's theory had the elegance of Ockham's razor, Bukharin's concept of the "unity of contradictions" in his theory of capitalist collapse was an overdetermined system of theoretical overkill that no doubt assuaged his impatience for the end. But perhaps Luxemburg's longer-run theory is the more relevant one – if capitalism is ever to collapse.

VI

One final word on Luxemburg's theory of catastrophic collapse, of which the Club of Rome's limits-to-growth thesis is a contemporary variation. As Norman Geras has convincingly demonstrated,[26]

Luxemburg's detractors, in their charge of mechanical fatalism, failed completely to understand the essence of her position. It was in the "or" of the "decline of civilization *or* the transition to socialism" and in the "Barbarism *or* Socialism" slogan of her 1916 *Junius Pamphlet* that the key to understanding Luxemburg lay. She was anything but a subscriber to Kautsky's notion of a mechanical dialectic (in his *Road to Power*). As Geras points out, Luxemburg equated barbarism with the collapse of capitalism – a collapse that, if unchallenged, would doom all civilization to extinction. The need for revolutionary activity was all the greater if extinction was to be avoided. The supersession of capitalism was a 'necessity' in the sense that without it we are all doomed, not that it would *inevitably* follow the collapse of capitalism. The closer imperialism gets to Luxemburg's theoretical limit of capital accumulation, the greater becomes the danger of a collapse into chaos – as will be argued below in describing Kissinger's reaction to the OPEC oil embargo. We are by no means out of the woods, and there is still much in Luxemburg's apocalyptic vision that deserves serious consideration.

At any rate, 'historical necessity' for Luxemburg did not mean 'determinism'.[27] As Geras observes, "There is more than one kind of necessity under the sun" and to pin the label of vulgar, mechanical Marxism on Luxemburg is to dishonor her and give the lie to the whole corpus of her political and radical activity – which in the end cost her her life.

3

The limitless accumulation of capital in postcapitalist society

I

One question remains to complete Rosa Luxemburg's analysis of the accumulation of capital. Assume we not only escape the 'barbarism' she so feared, but that somehow we also manage to achieve a *true* supersession of capitalism. That the Soviet Union is not a true supersession hardly requires argument. As early as 1932, in reviewing Marx's youthful 1844 *Paris Manuscripts,* Herbert Marcuse[1] characterized the Soviet Union as a system that had only replaced private property with 'universal' private property, a crude form of communism that was "merely the simple 'negation' of capitalism and as such exists on the same level as capitalism." In the terminology of the young Marx, Soviet labor is therefore just as 'alienated' and 'estranged' as capitalist labor; indeed, the Soviet Union is simply another form of capitalism. A more recent blast,[2] along similar lines, came upon the promulgation, with much fanfare, of the Soviet Union's new Constitution on June 4, 1977. China referred to it as a "fig leaf" to cover the betrayal of the proletariat by "a handful of bureaucrat-monopolist capitalists," a "cabal of revisionist renegades" who have usurped the proletariat and revived capitalism. From the Chinese point of view, the Soviet Union is a "bureaucrat-monopoly" version of the capitalist system where "the rich get richer and the poor poorer and class antagonism gets more pronounced than ever." A few days later they reminded Brezhnev, who has a vast collection of capitalist cars, of the fate of Louis XVI.

But what of a truly postcapitalist, classless society concerned only with the 'administration of things', not men? What would the accumulation of capital be like? Would any limit to capital accumulation exist, in fact or in theory? Would capital accumulation cease in a socialist society (implying a stationary state), or would it continue to be a driving force? With the exception of Luxemburg, this question has been studiously avoided by Marxists. The mature Marx of *Capital* had nothing to say about it, although some inferences can be drawn from

33

his more exuberant period of the 1844 *Manuscripts,* from the views he expressed in the *German Ideology,* and from the seven notebooks he filled up in the winter of 1857-8 (the *Grundrisse*) in preparation for Volume I of *Capital.*

Luxemburg's theory of capital accumulation under socialism will be presented first, followed by a critical account of Marx's dim, though supporting, version. This is not an area where much work has been done, and it has nothing to do with the type of planning practiced in the Soviet Union and the communist countries of Eastern Europe. It is principally a *theoretical* extrapolation of some of the basic ideas of Marx, although Marx himself bordered at times on total confusion.

According to Luxemburg, the profit motive acts as a *constraint* on capitalist accumulation and hence on growth. This is not to say that the rate of capitalist accumulation is low; it is not. But it is lower than it would or could be in the absence of the profit constraint. Apart from Luxemburg's argument that a capitalist is "interested in a machine only when the costs of production . . . amount to less than the wages of the workers it replaces,"[3] there is the restraining fear of obsolescence and the losses involved in too rapid a rate of technological change under monopoly capitalism. In a communist society, however, machinery will be substituted for labor "just as soon as it can save more human labour than is necessary for making it" (*Accumulation,* p. 322). In this liberated state, "rational-purposive action," to use Habermas's phrase, would have almost unbelievable results because, in Luxemburg's view, "the general use of machinery in the productive process will be put on a new economic basis" (p. 322). She continues (pp. 322-3; italics supplied):

> [R]ational scientific techniques can only be applied on the largest scale when the barriers of private ownership in land are abolished. This will result in an *immense* revolution . . . which will ultimately amount to a replacement of living labor, and which will enable us to tackle technical jobs *on a scale quite impossible under present day conditions.* . . . [I]f the capitalist profit motive is abolished and a social organization of labour introduced, the marginal use of the machine will suddenly be increased by the whole extent of the capitalist surplus value, so that an enormous field, not to be gauged as yet, will be open to *the triumphal march of the machine.* This would be tangible proof that the capitalist mode of production, alleged to spur on to the optimal technical development, in fact sets large social limits to technical progress, in the form

of the profit motive on which it is based. It would show that *as soon as these limits are abolished, technical progress will develop such a powerful drive that the technical marvels of capitalist production will be child's play in comparison.*

Hypertrophic socialism will have at last arrived. With the profit motive out of the way and the "triumphal march of the machine" assured, *"the progressive subjection of nature to social labour* becomes even more striking when production is organized solely with a view to human needs" (p. 323; italics supplied). Because in this classless society alienated labor will either not exist or be at a rock-bottom minimum, the domination of nature will be divorced from the domination of man, as man is objectified in his *free* labor. Pentheus will have at last successfully manacled the hands of Dionysus! There will be no theoretical necessity to limit the accumulation of capital in the classless society and therefore no Malthusian specter to limit the growth of population, as indeed many Marxists have argued in the past. Due to the constraints of the profit motive on capital accumulation, it would appear that capitalism must experience a lower rate of economic growth under conditions of alienated and reified labor than would be the case in a liberated communist society.

This theme was picked up more recently by the exiled Czech Marxist, Ota Šik.[4] Although he doubted that alienation would totally disappear even in a 'truly' communist society, at least the capitalist form of alienated work would be absent. Because capitalist alienation acts "as a *mounting* barrier to economically effective production," relatively unalienated socialist labor will "*ensure more effective growth of the productive forces* than [is] possible under capitalism," for a "more effective development of productive forces" will be feasible and hence a higher rate of economic growth. Surprisingly, some capitalists are willing to concede the point, even for a not-so-liberated communist society. When Khrushshev launched his "peaceful coexistence" campaign during the 1960s, panic broke out at the Rand Corporation. It admitted the Soviet Union's ability to sustain a higher growth rate and argued for a substitution of the "battle of the budgets" for the "battle of the GNPs" – a rather quaint way of arguing for an accelerated arms race. The reason why the United States could not, and should not, try to match the higher growth rate of the Soviet Union, according to Rand and its followers, was that each percentage-point increase in the U.S. growth rate would require such an inordinate increase in the ratio of net investment to GNP that the capitalist system would be wrecked in the process.[5]

II

From Luxemburg's point of view, at any rate, all 'good' theoretical Marxists must posit a necessary and ultimate limit to capitalist accumulation although denying it in principle for the classless society. It would be interesting to see if some support for Luxemburg's position can be found in the writings of Karl Marx himself. It is not easy to do so because, in the whole corpus of his writings, Marx had little to say about what a truly communist society would look like. The matter is complicated by the fact that although it is fashionable, nowadays, to tout the unity of Marx's thought from the youthful romanticism of his *Paris Manuscripts* to his more mature writing in *Capital,* there is a yawning gulf between the two, particularly in the development of his thought on the nature of historical materialism.[6] We begin with his 1844 *Manuscripts.*

The young Marx made frequent use of such terms as 'alienation', 'estrangement', 'supersession', 'objectification', 'species-being', and 'exteriorization' – terms that virtually disappeared from his more mature writings.[7] Under the deep influence of Hegel's *Phenomenology of Mind* and Feuerbach's *Essence of Christianity,* Marx viewed the relationship of man and nature, in a nonalienated state, in terms of their *unity.* In his *Paris Manuscripts,* Man was a "species-being" consciously aware of himself, with labor as "man's act of self-genesis" (p. 188). Nature was no more than *"man's inorganic body – nature, that is, in so far as it is not itself the human body"* (p. 112). By appropriating his "inorganic body," man lived on nature, which implied that nature was that part of his *body* "with which he must remain in continuous interchange if he is not to die" (p. 112).

Labor, as the act of appropriating that other part of his body, is one of the two basic ontological categories of Marx – the other being the "realm of necessity," which does not appear until the *Grundrisse,* in opposition to his 1844 writings. In the objectification of his species-being, man engages in production, and it is in this act of production that "nature appears as *his* work and his reality" (p. 114). To put the matter even more strongly, "nature is linked to itself" through man's labor in the act of production. It is when this unity of man and nature is destroyed by capitalism that labor becomes reified and estranged and made to appear as something external to man – as an object and a commodity. Combining it with labor's past expenditures of time (i.e., *Capital*), capital based on private property serves as the basis for all accumulation.

"Accumulation," wrote Marx, "where private property prevails, is the *concentration* of capital in the hands of the few, it is the general and inevitable consequence if capital is left to follow its own natural course" (p. 83; Marx's italics). Accumulation becomes possible at first only because of capitalist competition, but as factory labor becomes the predominant form of work, requiring larger amounts of fixed capital in the more advanced stages of capitalism, the small capitalist is squeezed out and "the accumulation of capital is . . . accompanied by *a proportional concentration and simplification of fixed capital*" (p. 86; italics supplied). This concentration and simplification of capital can be taken to represent the technological progress that Marx was later to emphasize in the *Grundrisse* as *the* major factor in capitalist production, with the progressive displacement of labor by capital leading to still greater accumulations of surplus value – the 'realization' of which Luxemburg later saw as the insoluble problem of advanced capitalism.

In summary form, competition leads to accumulation which leads to industrialization. Industrialization, however, proceeds on the basis of economies of scale and a greater concentration of increasingly sophisticated fixed capital (technological change), which in turn leads to a falling rate of profit, the decline of competition, and huge concentrations of power in the hands of fewer and fewer surviving capitalists. But this accumulation of capital is based on the central theme of Marx's 1844 *Manuscripts – private property.* It is private property that is the cause of alienated and estranged labor; the destruction of objectified labor and man's unity with that other part of his body, inorganic nature.

Given the historical conditions of a capitalism based on private property and accumulation, the young Marx had a jaundiced view of the division of labor, which followed from the big capitalists' introduction of "some kind of organization of the instruments of labor" and their consequent ability, by virtue of the "proportionate concentration and simplification of fixed capital . . . to combine different branches of production" (pp. 86, 91) along more effective lines. "The division of labor," wrote Marx, "is . . . nothing else but the *estranged, alienated* position of human activity" (p. 159; Marx's italics). Writing to himself in a quick, staccato shorthand, we find the following on page 164 of the *Manuscripts* (second italics supplied):

> Human labor is simply *mechanical motion:* the main work is done by the material properties of the objects. The fewest possible operations must be apportioned to any one individual. *Splitting up labor and concentration of capital;* the nothingness of individual production and the production of wealth in large quantities. Meaning of private property within the division of labor.

Two pages earlier he wrote: "Division of labor . . . reduces the *ability of each person* taken *individually*" (Marx's italics). It was this division of labor that became the "major driving force in the production of wealth as soon as *labor* was recognized as *the essence of private property* – i.e., about *the estranged and alienated form* of human activity as an activity of the species" (p. 159; Marx's italics). Marx, moreover, was explicit in linking the division of labor with the accumulation of capital. "The whole of modern political economy," he declared, "agrees . . . that *the . . . division of labor and accumulation of capital mutually determine each other*" (p. 162; italics supplied). It would appear, therefore, that in the supersession of capitalism the division of labor and hence the accumulation of capital upon which it is based would disappear – contrary to Luxemburg's analysis. A quotation from the *German Ideology* drives home the point:

> [I]n a communist society, where nobody has one exclusive sphere of activity, but each can become accomplished in any branch he wishes, society regulates the general production and thus makes it possible for me to do one thing today and another tomorrow, to hunt in the morning, fish in the afternoon, rear cattle in the evening, criticize after dinner, just as I have a mind, without ever becoming hunter, fisherman, shepherd or critic.[8]

One wonders what would happen to the higher rate of accumulation and economic growth that Luxemburg foresaw in a communist society, but then this was the youthful, more romantic Marx, who saw work in postcapitalist society, à la Fourier, as fun and games. The young Marx was forced to this conclusion by equating the division of labor with the production of wealth and the production of wealth with the accumulation of capital, for the latter is a necessary precondition for the production of wealth. But, further, because the division of labor is based on private property and the private ownership of the accumulating means of production, it is also the source of reified, alienated labor and the divorce of man from his inorganic body, nature. The end result is the identification of the division of labor with its exploitation and estrangement in a capitalist society. Therefore, if one is against estrangement, one must also be against the division of labor.

Marx's view of the process of production in the 1844 *Manuscripts,* however, provides an alternate approach to the problem of accumulation that, on the surface, seems to be in contradiction to his analysis of the division of labor.* Natural science had "invaded and transformed human life ... through the medium of industry." Indeed, to Marx industry was "the *actual,* historical relationship of nature ... to man." As it develops through industry, nature becomes "the true *anthropological* nature." The essential powers of man "can only find their self-understanding in the science of the natural world in general" (p. 143; Marx's italics). Marx developed these seminal ideas further in the *Grundrisse,* where science and technology were linked with the accumulation of capital as the main productive force.

Although science and technology applied to the production process is a capitalist phenomenon, the development of capitalism was not to be seen as a pure historical accident, a matter of mere chance. As Marcuse pointed out in his 1932 analysis of the *Paris Manuscripts,*[9] "Objectification always carries with it a tendency towards reification and labour a tendency towards alienation, so that *reification and alienation are not merely chance factors.*" Indeed, the historical development of alienating capitalism will, in the end, with its rapid accumulation of capital based on the natural sciences, serve as the basis for man's ultimate liberation and the emancipation of human freedom from the realm of necessity (at least on the basis of the 1844 *Manuscripts,* for in the *Grundrisse* Marx was to change his tune on the possibility of going *beyond* necessity). Apart from this problem of depassing 'necessity', Marx was quite clear in the *Manuscripts.* The transformation of human life through the fusion of science and capitalist industry laid the ground for "human emancipation, although its immediate effect had to be the furthering of the dehumanization of man" (p. 143). Science and industry (and presumably the continued accumulation of capital) thus play a mediating role between man, as an historical animal, and his inorganic body, nature, and serve as the basis for man's final liberation from his externalized and antagonistic struggle with nature.

Perhaps the greatest significance of the 1844 *Manuscripts* lies in one of the very rare descriptions Marx ever gave of what a post-post-capitalist, communist society would look like. In keeping with his linkage of alienation with private property, Marx saw communism as "the *positive* transcendence of *private property,* as *human self-estrangement,* and therefore as the real *appropriation of the human essence*

*A possible explanation is that the manuscripts were just that – *manuscripts;* a collection of essays written over a six-month period in which a twenty-six-year-old Marx turned certain ideas over in his head and wrote notes to himself. They were a "search for clarification," not a finished, integrated product intended for publication.

by and for man; communism therefore as the complete return of man to himself as a *social* (i.e., human) being" (p. 135; Marx's italics). In a celebrated passage relating communism with humanism, Marx wrote (p. 135; second italics supplied):

> Communism, as a fully developed naturalism, equals humanism; it is the *genuine* resolution of the conflict between man and nature and between man and man – *the true resolution of the strife ... between freedom and necessity....* Communism is the riddle of history solved.

Within communist society, the unity of man with nature is restored and the "hostility" between man's "general consciousness" and his "real life" abolished. Universal harmony reigns supreme. But although "communism is the necessary pattern and the dynamic principle of the immediate future," it was *not* to be taken as *the* "goal of human development." On the contrary, the goal of human development is "the structure of human society," with communism as its exclusive means of attainment (p. 146). But we are still faced with the problem of accumulation within a communist society and for the resolution of this problem, along Rosa Luxemburg's line, the 1844 *Manuscripts* remain obscure and, at times, contradictory. For the solution we must turn to the *Grundrisse* of 1857–8.

III

For Luxemburg, the division of labor would have to continue if the accumulation of capital were to be the powerful and truly liberating force of a communist society. How else could the increasing organic composition of capital open up the path for "the triumphal march of the machine," with technical progress developing "such a powerful drive that the technical marvels of capitalist production [would] be child's play in comparison"? It is on this issue that the *Grundrisse* reverses Marx's earlier position on the division of labor. If capital accumulation, backed by science, is to be the dynamic liberating force of postcapitalist society, then the division of labor must of necessity have a critical role to play. Moreover, Marx's Hegelian notions of objectification and the unity of man and nature, and "the true resolution of the strife ... between freedom and necessity," would have to be modified. At some basic, irreducible level the "conflict between man and nature" would continue, the "triumphal march of the machine" notwithstanding. It is at this point that the "realm of necessity" makes its appearance as Marx's *second* ontological category.

The first ontological category, labor, continues to reign. In the *Manuscripts* we find: "The nobility of man shines upon us from their work-hardened bodies" (p. 155). In the *Grundrisse* labor is "the living, shaping fire" (p. 361). But in the *Grundrisse* and in Volume I of *Capital* nature is not now merely "the inorganic body of man"; instead, Marx posits a "metabolism" of man and nature[10] in which the conflict between man and nature is not resolved but *transformed*. In appropriating nature, man is governed by natural laws anterior to man and, as Marx argued in Volume I of *Capital*, "Man can only proceed in his production in the same way as nature herself, that is he can only alter the *forms* of the material." Man is now one of nature's forces, who in appropriating nature through social production determines his human nature *historically*. Indeed, in his *Poverty of Philosophy* Marx criticized Proudhon for failing to see "that all history is nothing but a continuous transformation of nature." But as Alfred Schmidt points out, the metabolism between man and nature implies, in Marx's words, an *"external nature imposed necessity."* As a consequence, Schmidt argues, the mature Marx sees that "historical reality itself ... is ruled by eternal categories which are relatively independent of all changes." This eternal nature-imposed necessity applies to *all* human forms of social organization in all their historical facticities. The eternal realm of necessity now precludes any 'unity' (in the 1844 sense) of man and nature in a communist society where freedom triumphs over necessity. The struggle with nature is endless. What is in the power of man to do is to end the form of capitalist alienation based on the private ownership of capital.

In *Anti-Dühring*, Engels foresaw "Humanity's leap from the realm of necessity into the realm of freedom" by the mere "seizure of the means of production by society." There will be a conscious mastery over nature. Marx's view in Volume III of *Capital* is quite different. Man is doomed to "wrestle with nature ... *under all forms of production."* Even if man should rationally order his interchange with nature, as in a communist society, "it nonetheless still remains a realm of necessity." [11] Engels notwithstanding, there can be no going beyond necessity. As Schmidt observes, "Human happiness is not simply proportional to the measure of man's technical mastery over nature, but ... depends very much on the social organization of that mastery.... For Engels, the socialization of the means of production solves the problem.... [For] Marx ... the realm of freedom does not simply replace that of necessity, but retains it as an inextinguishable internal moment." For Marx, the "basic prerequisite" for achieving the realm of true freedom was a "shortening of the working day," and this clearly has as a precondition the further development and con-tribution of science and technology to the process of production, be-yond and far above that pioneered by capitalism – as Luxemburg explained in an impassioned voice.

Schmidt emphasizes the "dialectical duality" of Marx's materialism, or transcendence in nontranscendence, with the reconciliation of freedom and necessity "on the basis of necessity" and, we might add, technology. Marx now made science and technology itself the major force of production in capitalist society, not labor. And as Luxemburg argued, it would continue to be so, to an even greater extent, in postcapitalist society – should we ever get there. But whether in a capitalist or socialist society, the conflict with nature will persist, as will alienation, to a greater or lesser degree. The total abolition of alienation, given the realm of necessity, implies a utopia that only the younger Marx could dream about. The older Marx was not a "philosophical optimist." In the opinion of Schmidt, Marx "deserves a place [along with Freud] in the tradition of the great European pessimists." Labor, that "living, shaping fire" has, as Marx observed in the *German Ideology,* "the curse on itself of being 'burdened' with matter." This is dramatically brought out in the *Grundrisse.*

What will labor be like in a postcapitalist society? True, it will be "attractive work" leading to the "individual's self-realization," but this "in no way means that it becomes mere fun, mere amusement, as Fourier conceives it. *Really free work . . .* is at the same time *. . . the most damned serious, the most intense exertion,* which appears in the production process not in a merely natural spontaneous form, but *as an activity regulating all the forces of nature"* (pp. 611–12; italics supplied). Poor Fourier got it again, 100 pages later in the *Grundrisse* (italics supplied):

> Labour cannot become play, as Fourier would like. . . . Free time . . . transform(s) its possessor into a different subject. This process is then both discipline, as regards the human being in the process of becoming; and at the same time, prac-tice [Ausubüng], *experimental science, materially creative and ob-jectifying science.*

Once again, we see Marx's preoccupation with science as a critical factor in the process of production. The accumulation of capital under its aegis will not only "redound to the benefit of emancipated labour"; more importantly, it is the very "condition of its emancipa-tion" (p. 701). But emancipated labor, or free labor, does not mean wallowing in polymorphous perversity. The biblical injunction "By the sweat of thy brow" still holds for the realm of necessity, given man's fallen estate into materiality. Capital itself, and particularly the accumulation of capital, is "despite itself, instrumental in creating the means of socially disposable time, in order to reduce the labour time for the whole of society to a diminishing minimum" (p. 708).

Under capitalism, capital accumulation has a dual tendency according to Marx: "to create disposable time" and "to convert it into surplus labour." Presumably, in postcapitalist society the two will be resolved, as in Luxemburg's vision, to increase further the rates of technological change and capital accumulation and thus the rate of growth to a startling level. The "saving of labor" and the "free time" that will ensue will be put to the service of even more productive power; it will *"react back* on the productive power of labour *as itself the greatest productive power"* (p. 711; italics supplied). Free labor's reaction back on the productive power of labor will be channeled through technically oriented trade schools, where natural sciences will be taught with practical instruction in their applications to the productive process. In Volume I of *Capital,* children would be fully developed as human beings but *also* "as one of the methods of adding to the efficiency of production."

It is clear that, unlike the *Manuscripts* of 1844, alienation is no longer simply a matter of the division of labor under capitalism. In Volume I of *Capital,* Marx no longer espouses the abolition of the division of labor as such, but rather "the abolition of the *old* division of labour."[12] The key difference between capitalist and true communist production is the absence not of alienation but of *exploitation.* Admittedly, the residual alienation, based on the continued division of labor, would be at a minimum in a communist society. Or, as in Marcuse's *Eros and Civilization,* the achievement-oriented reality principle of capitalism will be replaced by one that will obliterate *surplus* repression, leaving only a minimum, unavoidable *basic* repression due to the realm of necessity. But this basic repression is not a constant. It would be progressively reduced by the advances of technology and the accumulation of 'communist' capital. As Marx himself pointed out, the emancipation of labor would be based on the technology developed by the capitalist system. And as Luxemburg argued, the rate of capital accumulation under communism will boggle the mind. But there is always the possibility of 'barbarism' for Luxemburg, with no guaranty that the ultimate nightmare of capitalism will be avoided. In the words of Alfred Schmidt (p. 163):

> Today when men's technical possibilities have outstripped the dreams of the old Utopians many times over, it appears rather that these possibilities, negatively realized, have

changed into forces of destruction, and therefore, instead of bringing about an albeit humanly limited salvation, lead to total destruction, a grim parody of the transformation intended by Marx, in which Subject and Object are not reconciled, but annihilated.

Maybe, after all, Luxemburg's apocalyptic vision of catstrophe will prove more prescient than her vision of the 'good' society. But even if, by some miracle, we somehow got to her ideal communist society, we would still not be out of the woods for, according to Luxemburg, there can be no theoretical limit to capital accumulation or growth in a truly communist society. The sky is the limit, and her vision of communist accumulation could well allow us to hoist her on her own petard.

It bears repeating, however, that the increasing organic composition of capital and the tendency of a decreasing rate of capitalist profit, in Marx, implied a theory of capitalist crises. In no sense did Marx have a catastrophe theory of capitalism based on an excessive accumulation of capital. Only Luxemburg did. The downfall of capitalism would not be a technical matter of theory in Marx. Permanent capitalist crises do not exist, and no crisis in capitalism exists that cannot be solved by the capitalists. But from one crisis to another the amount and intensity of human suffering increases, and in the end it is this mounting suffering, or growing intolerance of suffering, that will bring down the system by raising the consciousness of the proletariat (who alone serve as the historical agents of change and revolution) to the appropriate level – assuming, of course, that in its historical development, capitalism does not co-opt the proletariat.

If, however, there are exogenous limits to capital accumulation that apply equally to both capitalist and communist societies (for example, the finiteness of the world's resources or ecological constraints on limitless capital accumulation), then it would seem to follow, on theoretical grounds, that catastrophe theory is more directly applicable to a classless, communist society than to a capitalist one. This is the ultimate irony: The restraint of the profit motive on capitalist accumulation that Luxemburg talked about would give capitalism more time! The "triumphal march of the machine" under communism at an as yet undreamed of and unimaginable rate would speed the classless society to an *earlier* catastrophic doom.

Of course, these are theoretical properties of the two systems, assuming the existence of a common exogenous constraint, and not necessarily predictions of the actual course of historical events in a world of rampant nationalism. There is no reason to believe that either type of society could learn to adjust properly to a finite economic universe. On the other hand, a blind submission to the imperative of economic growth could undo both in rather short order – with socialism's possibly quicker exhaustion of material resources the greater potential threat, in line with Luxemburg's analysis. One could argue that a communist society, being more humane and less profit driven, would adjust more intelligently to the realm of necessity and reduce its rate of capital accumulation to an accommodating level; but one would first have to get there for this to be a possibility. In the entire history of capitalism, so far, capitalism has shown a great capacity to adapt and to adjust to changing historical conditions, and as long as capitalism continues to be able to do so, communism becomes only the grandest of all utopian dreams. In that case, it would be better to turn to a realistic analysis of contemporary advanced capitalism and where it seems to be going.

PART II

Neo- and non-Marxian theories of advanced capitalism

4

The problem of capitalist legitimation

Social *reality* is tragically misshapen, intractable, and untidy. Social *theory* is not. It imposes order and clarity by forcing the 'facts' of social existence into preconceived ideological boxes – all in the name of objective science. Superficially, it appears that what separates one social theory from another is the way in which the same 'objective' facts are arranged and combined. But it is the underlying ideology that determines what a social fact is to begin with and then proceeds to arrange the ones it finds to be theoretically relevant and compatible in a certain order. Different theories, being different constructions of 'reality', have different objectives. Some seek to eternalize and thereby justify whatever *is,* while others seek to depass it to what *ought* to be. One thing all social theories have in common, however, is that they all, in time, become obsolete as historical events unfold along lines no theory could have possibly anticipated.

In a sense, all social theories specialize in predicting the past and having done so, in accordance with their own 'scientific' canons and thus to their own satisfaction, they then turn their theoretical axes 180 degrees into the future, falsifying themselves in the act. Then comes the problem of reconstruction, after the patchwork attempts of the theoretical diehards repeatedly fail. And so the process goes on and on, though by no means smoothly. For any major social theory with a large body of adherents, it is often a turbulent process that can turn ugly when the official custodians of the theory also happen to have the political power to back up their theoretical convictions. But as ugly as it may turn, the need to reconstitute social theories continues, and new formulations more relevant to their times continue to appear.

Capitalist theory went through its major overhaul in the form of the Keynesian revolution, which was tamed and captured by neoclassicists who transformed it into a mechanical model for capitalist problem solving. Marxian theory, on the other hand, went through its major upheaval shortly after the death of Engels, only to be similarly cap-

49

the revolutions of 1848 led to the replacement of traditional society by a *bürgerliche Gesellschaft.*

III

The arrival of capitalism on the historical scene is a very recent phenomenon going back, in its more modern form, to one's grandparents or one's great-grandparents at the most. Yet the productive and destructive forces it let loose were unparalleled in all of human existence and are still strongly reverberating in the present. Capitalism was the first form of socioeconomic organization to subordinate man's social relations to the economic sphere. It was the first to attempt a systematic subjegation of nature through science and to convert technology into *the* major productive force. It was the first to treat the world as prey and to institutionalize growth and limitless, self-propelling capital accumulation as its raison d'être. It was the first to use an ever-rising productive power to co-opt the masses, contrary to traditional Marxian thought, by raising real wages and the standard of living. Finally, and most important of all, it was the first to fuse science and ideology by making the scientific paradigm virtually indistinguishable from the political ideology that supports it; both, working in tandem, serve to legitimate and consolidate the capitalist structure of power.

In its initial, liberal phase, the legitimating theory of capitalism annihilated the concept of class and replaced it with atomized individuals subject to impersonal market forces. The movement now was from a subject–king to a labor–capital relationship. Political power was no longer based explicitly on class, as it was in traditional society. Production, on the other hand, depended on the relationship of capital to labor in competitive markets which, in turn, signified the "depoliticization of the class relationship and the anonymization of class domination."[2] The institution of the market, with its "exchange of equivalents," resulted in a bourgeois legitimation *from below;* that is, from the relations of production based on work. The political system, in other words, became justified in terms of a market-oriented work ethic.

From an economist's point of view, Habermas's theory of legitimation from below in liberal capitalism can be easily explained by reference to the neoclassical marginal productivity theory of distribution. The price of each factor input (capital and labor) is determined in a competitive market that cannot be manipulated or controlled by the factor involved. The capitalist, serving as *entrepreneur,* is the organizer of production and receives for his services 'normal' profits that are themselves competitively determined. He is also, in the short run, the

52

residual claimant to all revenues that exceed payments to capital and labor – if there are any. In the long run, however, the total product is fully accounted for, theoretically, by factor disbursements to capital and labor and to the capitalist as entrepreneur; there are no residual profits for the capitalist to claim. Competitive markets, in other words, in determining the prices of all factor inputs determine at the same time the distribution of the social product among the factors of production. Each factor input is rewarded strictly in terms of its *contribution* to total output. The rule for distribution was simple: From each according to his ability, to each according to his contribution.

As capital accumulation based on technological change proceeded at an increasing rate, capital's increasing contribution to total output was explicitly recognized and rewarded. But the entrepreneur, or capitalist, *owned* the capital employed in the productive process (the means of production other than labor) and was thus legally entitled to its increased earnings as well – property rights having been justified by the theory of natural rights. Capitalist profits were thus seen as the wages of entrepreneurship to which the earnings of capital are added by legal sanction, thereby skewing the distribution of income in favor of the capitalist class.

The rule of distribution under liberal capitalism therefore effectively ruled out an equality of distribution, or a distribution according to need. From the Marxian point of view, however, capital was looked upon as congealed labor time; for it was labor that produced the capital that helped produce the output that everyone consumed in each production time period. And it would seem to follow that labor should therefore be entitled to capital's share of the total output. But this contradicted the liberal capitalist notion of property rights as applied to the nonlabor means of production. Capital, after all, had its own existence and its own reward. In what sense, then, could marginal productivity theory be the basis of legitimation from below and a depoliticized relation between capitalists and workers?

The actual truth or falsity of marginal productivity theory is totally beside the point. It is an irrelevant issue for liberal capitalism and arguments over its applicability, let alone truth content, even today, are a waste of everyone's time. Liberal capitalism simply brushed aside the ethical problem of distribution by raising the 'law' of marginal productivity to the level of a seemingly 'scientific' and therefore unchallengeable 'truth'. In doing so, it depoliticized the relations of labor and capital by reducing both to reified inputs in a market system. The class structure of society thus disappeared from view as liberal capitalism completed its 'legitimation from below'. The essential point is that marginal productivity theory achieved its legitimating power by the rise of the empirico-analytical methodology of the natural sciences. Logical 'validity' was elevated to the realm of scientific 'truth', with the entire corpus of bourgeois theory (of which marginal productivity theory was only a part) playing a *functional* role in the legitimation of liberal capitalism.

IV

The legitimating power of bourgeois ideology, according to Georg Lukács,[3] found "refuge in the methods of natural science," where all phenomena were reduced "to their purely quantitative essence" and their "expression in numbers and numerical relations." It was a "blinkered empiricism" that refused, in the name of abstract science, to "take account of the historical character of . . . facts." The ideological biases of bourgeois science took on "the appearance of timeless, eternal categories valid for all social formations." Some further quotations from Lukács* can be profitably used to explain Habermas's theory of "legitimation from below":

> [I]t is a matter of life and death [for liberal capitalism] to understand its own system of production in terms of eternally valid categories: *it must think of capitalism as being predestined to eternal survival by the eternal laws of nature over reason.* . . . By this stroke the objective economic antagonism as expressed in the class struggle evaporates leaving only a conflict between the individual and society.

> Man finds himself confronted by purely natural relations of social forms mystified into natural relations. *They appear to be fixed and immutable entities which can be manipulated and even comprehended, but never overthrown.*

> The starting point and goal [of bourgeois thought] are always, if not always consciously, an apologia for the existing order of things or at least a proof of their immutability. [italics supplied]

The critical fusion of science and ideology, in other words, provided the legitimating power of capitalism by basing the 'laws' of

---

*It is puzzling to find almost no references to either Georg Lukács or Rosa Luxemburg in the writings of Habermas and his followers. Possible reasons for this are the threat Lukács poses for Habermas's theory of communicative ethics and the contempt that Luxemburg had for seminar Marxists. I will return to this below, in the concluding chapter.

bourgeois economics on "the unalterable foundations of 'science'."
The fact/value separation of contemporary economic theory is very
much to the point. Unlike linguistic or biological structuralism, in the
social sciences there are only phenomena. Insofar as a noumenal sub-
structure exists, if indeed it does, it acts and is acted upon by the
phenomenal world. The two interact like "a pair of stars waltzing
around one another under the attraction of their mutual gravity."
The fact/value separation of the scientific paradigm in economics is
apparently oblivious of this possibility. It treats the noumenal world as
a hard rock buried under the shifting sands of an unstable and ever-
changing phenomenal world waiting only to be uncovered. In this
view, the pragmatic dependence of praxis on theory emerges as the
technical problem-solving application of 'scientific' economic
theories.[4] Science is thus transformed into an ideology of the status
quo. Or, in Lukács's terms, a mere point in historical time is raised to
the empyreal heights of universal abstraction, with all prior history
seen as the inevitable culmination in the static splendor of that one
point beyond which all future history ceases to exist. Science and
technology thus become the legitimating force of bourgeois society as
well as the determinant force in the productive process, as Marx himself recognized in the *Grundrisse*.

In summary, liberal capitalism's legitimating power from below was
based on the *depoliticized* work ethic of a competitive market system
raised by boureois theory to the level of natural law. Early capitalist
economists were even prepared to apply the laws of economics to the
entire man, not just to his labor, and to reduce the very essence of
man to the equivalent of a machine. Writing in 1826, McCulloch took
the plunge:

> Man is as much the *produce of labor* as any of the machines
> constructed by his agency: and . . . ought to be considered in
> precisely the same point of view. Every individual who has
> arrived at maturity . . . may, with perfect propriety, be viewed
> as a machine which it has cost 20 years of assiduous attention
> and the expenditure of a considerable capital to construct.[5]

Man, by the eternal laws of economics, was to be seen simply as a
machine operating alongside other machines in the work process.
And his earnings, according to marginal productivity theory, were no
differently determined than the earnings of any other machine. This
theory of distribution based on each machine's contribution to total
output was usually stated in abstract theoretical terms. On occasion,
however, it was not. Herbert Spencer, one of the major nineteenth-

century exponents of liberal capitalism, was not one to shy away from the raw human implications of the economic 'laws' of liberal capitalism as applied to the human 'machine':

> The command, "if any could not work neither should he eat," is simply a Christian enunciation of that universal law of nature under which life has reached its present height – the law that a creature not energetic enough to maintain itself must die.

After that, one must admire the subtlety of the marginal productivity theory of distribution!

To summarize: In marginal productivity theory, where each contributes according to his ability and is rewarded in keeping with his contribution, the capitalist by natural right appropriates the earnings of capital; that is, by virtue of his ownership of the dead means of production which, in turn, is sanctioned by the legal process. Given the role of capital in technological progress, the obsolescence of Marx's labor theory of value could very well be based on the main point of Baranovsky's argument that Luxemburg conceded. The earnings of capital, therefore, are not simply a matter of expropriating the surplus value of labor; they are more directly dependent on the rate of economic growth and the technological change upon which it is based. It would seem, according to Habermas's argument, that it is dynamic growth, and the exploitation and application of privately owned capital to achieve it, that is the driving force of capitalism and not the exploitation of labor or the expropriation of labor's surplus value.

But the flaw in liberal capitalism was to be found in what Habermas calls its "steering mechanism"; its inability to stave off periodic economic crises that undermined its legitimating power. Class antagonisms resurfaced and were *re*politicized due to "the patterns of a *crisis-ridden course of economic growth.*"[6] These recurrent economic crises of liberal capitalism, moreover, were transformed into social crises, which unmasked "the opposition of social classes" and provided "a practical critique of ideology of the market's pretensions to be free of power."[7] The problems of liberal capitalism, in short, were "structurally insoluble system contradictions or steering problems."[8] Until recently, the legitimation crisis of liberal capitalism was 're-solved' by its successor, advanced capitalism. Advanced capitalism compressed the systemic crises of liberal capitalism within a narrower, politically tolerable band, while maintaining, at the same time, the legitimating force of economic growth. The question now is whether it can continue to do so in a finite economic universe where growth itself has become the problematic.

V

Habermas's theory of advanced capitalism can be briefly summarized. The process of accumulation takes place in highly concentrated markets. The small capitalist is replaced by large oligopolistic and multinational corporations, with the state entering the system in a compensatory way when "functional gaps" develop. The movement this time is from a capital–labor to a capital–political relationship. But advanced capitalism, with the symbiotic relationship between the concentrated sector and the state, is not without its market-steering mechanism. Investment decisions are still made on a private basis "according to criteria of company profits."

Habermas uses a three-sector model: the competitive and oligopolistic sectors plus the government sector. This type of model is much in vogue, and there is no point in detailing its characteristics. More generally, it is in the capital-intensive oligopolistic sector where "rapid advances in production" take place. The labor-intensive competitive sector is peripheral and parasitically dependent upon the oligopolistic sector. Many investment decisions, moreover, are made "almost without regard for the market," especially in such industries as defense and aerospace.

The public sector, on the other hand, represents the administrative system of the state. It engages in what Habermas calls, somewhat incorrectly, "global planning." Its purpose is to assure, insofar as possible, a dynamic long-term growth path at relatively full employment. But the global planning of the state is constrained by the private sphere; it is not allowed to make direct decisions concerning the rate of private investment. The raison d'être of the state administrative system is *crisis avoidance,* not planning in the full sense of the term. It restricts its operations to influencing private decisions *within* the boundary conditions of the system. What Habermas is obviously talking about is the problem-solving techniques of 'bastard' or 'vulgar' Keynesianism.

All this is all too familiar. Where Habermas adds something of importance to his analysis is in his description of the "legitimation system" of advanced capitalism. The recurrent crises of liberal capitalism shattered the system's ability to legitimate from below. As a result, the economic and political systems were combined in order to cope with the repoliticization of the relations of production. The pseudoscientific 'laws' of liberal capitalism had been discredited in the Great Depression of the 1930s. Advanced capitalism therefore instituted a system of formal democracy based on the pluralist paradigm in order to suppress from popular consciousness "the contradiction between administratively socialized production and the continued private appropriation and use of surplus value."[9] The administrative system of the state thereby succeeded in making itself "sufficiently independent of legitimating will-formation"; that is, administrative decisions by administrative technocrats were made independent of the "specific motives of . . . citizens." The legitimation process of advanced capitalism, in short, "elicits generalized motives – that is, diffuse mass loyalty – but avoids participation." What we have is a depoliticized public realm combined with "civic privatism." This structural depoliticization is justified either by "democratic élite theories" or by "technocratic systems theories."

The repoliticization of the relations of production in advanced capitalism, with its threat of rekindled class antagonisms, is avoided and suppressed by the privatization of its citizens – provided the technocrats do their job of crisis avoidance tolerably well. The repoliticization of the relations of production are offset by what can be more appropriately called domestic counterinsurgency programs. Functioning properly, class antagonisms remain latent because the system is able to co-opt labor by a crisis-free growth path disturbed only by mild recessions followed by quick recoveries.[10]

Writing before the post–Vietnam War depression of the 1970s, Habermas, though doubtful of the long-run viability of advanced capitalism, was not willing completely to "exclude the possibility that economic crisis can be permanently avoided." Yet he felt that advanced capitalism would find itself in a vulnerable position if its administrative ability were to realize what he calls a *rationality deficit* in public administration; that is, if its gyroscope were to malfunction. Were this to happen, a *legitimation deficit* would follow the output crisis of the rationality deficit, leading to a deterioration of the *normative* basis of its overall system of legitimation. The relations of production would then be repoliticized in the consciousness of the people, and the class struggle would be transformed from its dormant state into a threatening class confrontation. The reason for this possible breakdown of capitalism, its 'internal contradiction', he attributed to the *limited* ability of the administrative apparatus to function at an optimal level. Advanced capitalism, in other words, is essentially *unplanned*, with the boundary conditions of the system unable to expand without bringing the whole system into question. In Habermas's words:

On the one hand, in advanced capitalism the need for administrative planning to secure the realization of capital grows. On the other hand, *the private autonomous disposition of the means of production demands a limitation to state intervention and prohibits planned coordination of the contradictory interests of individual capitalists.* . . . The problems of an economic system controlled by the imperatives of capital realization cannot be taken over into the administratively controlled domain, and processed there, without the spread of orientations alien to the structure.[11]

It is this rationality deficit in a bounded, unplanned, advanced capitalism that generates the legitimation deficit and the withdrawal of support by the now consciously repoliticized masses. Its normative basis, under these conditions, is shattered. The substitution of purposive-rational actions by the state for the market functions of liberal capitalism is bound to give rise to a rationality deficit because of "the *unconscious* character of the overall economic process"; that is, because of the "strict limitations imposed on state manipulation" by the capitalists themselves.[12] The property basis of capitalism, for one thing, is sacrosanct. It is a boundary condition that cannot be crossed by the state – according to Habermas. And there are strict limits to tampering with private investment decisions as well.

Because the very survival of capitalism depends uniquely on unlimited capital accumulation and on continuous economic growth for its legitimation, it is the *necessarily* unplanned nature of advanced capitalism that will most likely lead to its eventual downfall. From Habermas's point of view, the adaptability and flexibility of capitalism are fatally limited by the inflexible boundary conditions of the system.[13]

The "limited maneuvering capability of the state apparatus" is the critical point in Habermas's exposition on the 'inner contradiction' of advanced capitalism. The crisis of capitalism is due to the

growing socialization of production still adjusted to private ends [which] brings with it unfulfillable – because paradoxical – demands on the state apparatus. On the one hand, the state is supposed to act as a collective capitalist. On the other hand, competing individual capitalists cannot form or carry through a collective will *as long as freedom of investment is not eliminated.* Thus arise the mutually contradictory imperatives of expanding the planning capacity of the state with the aim of a collective-capitalist planning and, yet, *blocking precisely this ex-*

59

pansion, which would threaten the continued existence of capitalism.[14]

Again, in Habermas's view, the very survival of capitalism is contingent on its ability to realize an adequate rate of economic growth and the wants needed to sustain it. Its ability to do so, however, becomes progressively more problematical as long as the purposive-rational actions of the state remain unplanned and as long as capitalism must redistribute income to the *disenfranchised* lumpenproletariat in order to maintain the stability of the system; thereby affecting the rate of growth which, according to Habermas, is so critical to the system's very survival.

VI

The essence of Habermas's argument is that capitalism depends on unlimited capital accumulation and growth for its legitimation. The problem of advanced capitalism is that investment, or increases in the means of production (the stock of capital), is largely a private matter in which the state plays no direct role. Its role is limited to such indirect means as accelerated depreciation, tax credits on new investment, and reductions in corporate income taxes – all of which serve to increase the cash flow to corporations with no guaranty that it will be used to expand the productive base of capitalism. Or, the state may try to influence investment decisions even more indirectly by working on consumer expenditures via personal income tax changes, transfer payments, and the like. The role of the state is limited by the boundary conditions of advanced capitalism to influencing the environment within which private decisions are made, without interfering in any direct way with the functioning of the capitalist economy. This is, in short, the Keynesian compensatory, problem-solving approach to capitalist crises.

Habermas attributes the exclusion of direct state actions in the investment sphere to the boundary conditions of capitalism. The 'global planning' of the state is therefore limited to indirect crisis-avoidance functions which, given the 'freedom to invest' in the private sector, it is unable to realize optimally because truly effective planning would violate the boundary conditions of advanced capitalism. It is this supposed inflexibility of boundary conditions that leads, in Habermas's opinion, to inadequate or unstable growth paths that in turn lead to periodic crises, the loss of legitimation, and the repoliticization of the masses. It has all the appearances of a forced argument in which advanced capitalism has built within it certain 'inherent' contradictions that must ultimately lead to its destruction. The state's inability to guaranty the optimal rate of capital accumulation precludes the co-optation and privatization of the masses and therefore results in the breakdown of capitalism. The argument takes on a *mechanical* aspect that one would expect from a 'systems analysis' approach. Habermas nevertheless remains firmly within the Marxian framework. Yet his is a neo-Marxian approach to capitalism, in that it substitutes technology for the labor theory of value and recasts the class struggle in a Weberian legitimation context of depoliticization followed by repoliticization when inflexible boundary conditions preclude effective state participation in the economy.

Habermas has overstated his case and has underestimated the ability of capitalism to survive and adapt within its boundary conditions, and even to change them if necessary in order to accommodate itself to a world where unlimited capital accumulation has itself become the problematic. The issue of capitalist adaptability to changing external conditions will be covered in the next chapter. For now, the earlier arguments of Luxemburg will be recast in terms of modern growth theory and applied to Habermas's analysis of capitalist crises and the ways in which the state can indeed stave off its inherent contradictions *within* capitalism's boundary conditions, as Habermas sees them.

Luxemburg, as we have already seen, was one of the few Marxists to raise the issue of inadequate effective demand as a key to understanding the capitalist system. Her theory of capital accumulation and imperialism, however, was designed to explain how capitalism avoided the dénouement of its own inherent contradictions by postponing it into the future, though the day of reckoning (too late for her critics) was sure to come. Putting her catastrophe theory to the side for the moment, her theory of capital accumulation can be put on a more modern footing by recasting it in terms of net investment, or the addition to the stock of capital over time after due allowance has been made for physical depreciation. Use will be made of a highly simplified Keynesian growth model that brings in the longer-term supply side. Although it is a one-sector, classless formulation of effective demand, and has other shortcomings as well, it serves to push unnecessary complexities aside and to focus on a fundamental problem of capitalism simply and directly – especially with regard to Michal Kalecki's concern over the function of armament expenditures in a capitalist society.

To begin with, the problem of effective demand is basically a demand–supply relationship. An insufficiency of effective demand exists when the aggregate demand of consumers for goods and of producers for the means of production is not enough to absorb the aggregate supply of consumers' and producers' goods generated by the capitalist system – thus leading to an unemployment crisis and idle capacity which, if serious enough, *and in the absence of effective countermeasures by the state,* could lead to a full-blown legitimation crisis. An argument can easily be made that even if capitalism were to achieve full employment in the short run by the optimal combination of monetary and fiscal policy, it would nevertheless have an inherent bias, in time of peace, toward chronic deflation which, if left alone, would jeopardize the continued existence of capitalism. The nub of the problem is the 'dual character' of investment.[15] The ability of net investment to generate purchasing power is exceeded by its ability to produce goods, thus leading to a chronic state of excess supply resulting in deflation and unemployment, unless some very special and fortuitous conditions are met. To understand fully the nature of the problem, each side of the investment function can be looked upon separately and then brought together.

Aggregate demand increases by some multiple of the *increase* in investment. If we let ΔD represent the increase in aggregate demand (or income), ΔI the increase in net investment, and k the multiplier, we get

$$\Delta D = k\Delta I$$

The multiplier (k) determines the amount by which aggregate demand will increase as a result of an increase in net investment. It is dependent on the average and marginal propensities to save, which are assumed to be equal; that is, the multiplier depends on the proportion of aggregate income that will be saved and not spent on consumers' goods. If income should increase, say, by $100 billion (American billion) in real terms (adjusted for price-level changes) and $20 billion are not spent, then the 'propensity to save' is 20 percent or $1/5$. The multiplier is the *reciprocal* of this propensity to save, or 5. Therefore, aggregate demand will increase by five times the increase in net investment. Letting α represent the propensity to save, the increase in aggregate effective demand due to an increase in net investment can be rewritten as:

$$\Delta D = \frac{1}{\alpha} \Delta I$$

The important point is that aggregate demand increases by a multiple ($1/\alpha$) of the *increase* in net investment (ΔI).

Aggregate supply, on the other hand, is some multiple of *total* net investment (I). The supply multiplier is quite different from the demand multiplier. It is dependent on what is called the capital/output ratio (K/Q). If it takes $2 of capital (K) to produce $1 of output (Q), for example, it follows that for each dollar of capital 50¢ worth of output is produced. The *average productivity of capital* is therefore the reciprocal of the capital/output ratio, or Q/K = ½. Suppose total net investment in any one year is $50 billion (American billion). Then, given the average productivity of capital (Q/K = σ) at ½ or 50¢, the productive capacity of the economy, and hence aggregate supply, will increase by ½ of $50 billion, or by $25 billion. This relationship can be written as:

$$\Delta S = \sigma I$$

Unlike aggregate demand, which increases by some multiple of the *increase* in net investment, aggregate supply increases by some multiple of *total* net investment.

Suppose, to begin with, aggregate demand is initially equal to aggregate supply at full employment; that is, D – S. Capitalism, if it is to maintain its legitimacy through co-optation, must accumulate capital in order to grow. Indeed, as Marxists, neo-Marxists, and capitalist economists maintain, the key to capitalism is unlimited capital accumulation and growth. Without it, it is argued, capitalism is seriously compromised. The basic questions is, given a full employment equilibrium *to begin with,* at what rate must net investment flow in order to *maintain* full employment over time? To find this equilibrium rate of growth we equate ΔD with ΔS:

$$\Delta D = \Delta S$$

$$\Delta I \cdot \frac{1}{\alpha} = I\sigma$$

$$\frac{\Delta I}{I} = \alpha\sigma$$

That is, the equilibrium *rate* of capital accumulation ($\Delta I/I$) is determined by the product of the propensity to save and the supply multiplier.

At any growth rate smaller than $\alpha\sigma$, aggregate supply will exceed aggregate demand, and deflation and unemployment will set in as a result of an insufficiency of effective demand. Capitalism is on an exhausting treadmill: It must continuously run at a constant rate in order to stand still! If it pauses or even falters for a second, it will be dragged back into unemployment. For example, suppose that capitalism were to maintain net investment at a high level of $100 billion (American billion) each year. The productive capacity of the economy would continue to spew out $50 billion worth of additional goods each year, given an average productivity of capital of ½. But because net investment is constant (there being no increase in net investment), $\Delta I = 0$. On the demand side, therefore, $\Delta I \cdot 1/\alpha = 0$. There is no increase in aggregate effective demand to absorb the $50 billion of additional goods each year from the supply side, and *all* of Iσ adds up to an excess of aggregate supply. The capitalist economy must therefore implode.

If, on the other hand, net investment should for any reason *fall* to $80 billion (American billion) and be maintained at that lower level, the annual addition to aggregate supply would now be $40 billion instead of $50 billion. But aggregate demand would now not only be unable to buy the $40 billion worth of goods, it would also decrease its earlier level of consumption because ΔI is now *negative* and effective demand would actually *fall*, thereby exacerbating the excess supply situation; matters would go from bad to worse. Finally, even if net investment should increase each year, but at a rate less than the required $\alpha\sigma$ rate, the increase in aggregate effective demand would not be enough to absorb all the increase in aggregate supply, and deflation would set in.

In short, capitalism cannot allow investment to fall, nor is the maintenance of investment at a high level enough. It must grow at a constant rate determined by the propensity to save and the average productivity of capital. There is no built-in automatic mechanism in capitalism that assures an equilibrium rate of growth at full employment. Indeed, its momentary achievement would be a matter of pure happenstance. It is virtually impossible for capitalism to meet this requirement if investment, according to Habermas, is strictly a private matter, with the boundary conditions of capitalism forestalling any effective direct planning role by the state. The problem of capitalism is to be found in the 'dual character' of investment: It increases productive capacity by the full amount of net investment while increasing effective demand only by the increment of net investment. It is here that the inherent 'internal contradiction' of capitalism is to be found – *in peacetime*. In Evsey Domar's words, the problem is that

> the whole body of investment, so to speak, increases productive capacity, but only its very top – the increment – increases [effective demand]. . . . [P]rivate capitalist society . . . finds itself in a serious dilemma: if sufficient investment is not forthcoming today, unemployment will be here today. But if enough is invested today, still more will be needed tomor-

row. . . . Indeed, *it is difficult enough to keep investment at some reasonable level, but the requirement that it always be rising is not likely to be met for any considerable period of time.*[16]

The inherent tendency of advanced capitalism is, therefore, toward deflation and, in Habermasian terms, capitalism in inexorably headed for a legitimation crisis. Both Domar and Habermas, like Luxemburg in her theory of capital accumulation, must somehow explain why capitalism has not yet collapsed. Part of the answer, at least, must be that peace has not been the 'normal' long-run state of affairs under capitalism. It took World War II to get Western capitalism out of the morass of the Great Depression. And, in the post–World War II period, the Cold War, the Korean War, and the Vietnam War served to overstimulate capitalism in the United States and hence the other advanced capitalist countries as well. When relative peace did come in the 1960s after the Korean War and in the 1970s after the Vietnam War, American capitalism sagged as one would have expected on the basis of Domar's analysis. Another part of the explanation must be that the state in advanced capitalist society did act in a compensatory way, however sporadically and with varying degrees of effectiveness.

As for the second explanation, advanced capitalism did learn some lessons from the problems of liberal capitalism. The 1930s collapse and its culmination in World War II were sufficient to induce a change in capitalism's boundary conditions along lines prescribed by Keynesian theory – itself a product of the Great Depression. Capitalists accepted a greater role for the state. They agreed to put a floor under capitalism sufficient to sustain the legitimating power of capitalism *without moving to a permanent state of full employment.* This wasn't a deficiency inherent in capitalism, as Habermas would have it; it was a deliberate policy objective. The goal was to keep unemployment at *politically* tolerable levels without compromising the basic interests of the capitalist class as a whole. It had nothing to do with 'inflexible boundary conditions' based on noninterference with the private investment market.

Michal Kalecki brought this out forcibly in his political theory of the trade cycle.[17] The political problem of maintaining full employment, according to Kalecki, lay in the opposition of the capitalist class to government interference in the economy in general and their fear of "the social and political changes resulting from the *maintenance* of full employment." The main fear of full employment was that it would remove the "fear of the sack" as a disciplinary force. But the greater fear was the threat posed to capitalism by severe unemployment. The taming of Keynesian theory along more conservative lines was the end result. Capitalists would allow only those indirect fiscal and monetary measures that would stimulate private investment or underwrite consumption expenditures through reductions in taxes. Deficit financing would be tolerated to prevent massive layoffs but not to keep the economy at a full employment level. In an upswing, calls for 'fiscal prudence', a 'sound dollar', and a 'balanced budget' would serve to reverse the stimulating effects of deficit spending and abort the boom *before* full employment was reached. The final result is *submerged peaks* below the full employment potential and the substitution of mild 'recessions' for full-blown 'depressions' while unemployment is maintained at the *maximum* politically tolerable level. In Habermasian terms, although Habermas himself does not see it this way, the crisis-avoidance applications of rational-purposive actions by the state are to be limited to the minimum level compatible with the continuation of capitalism as a viable system; that is, at a level just sufficient to sustain the legitimation of capitalism.[18]

In this context, the function and responsibility of the state to maintain the credibility and legitimacy of capitalism does not require that it solve the problem of the trade cycle completely or maintain the economy at full employment. On the contrary, its apparent function is to dampen the amplitude of the trade cycle by putting a floor under the capitalist system while peaking the economy below its full employment potential. Keynes foresaw this in his *General Theory* in 1936:

> [T]he outstanding feature of our actual experience [is] . . . that we oscillate, avoiding the gravest extremes of fluctuation in employment and in prices in both directions, round an intermediate position appreciably below full employment and appreciably above the minimum employment *a decline below which would endanger life*.[19]

And, we might add, below which the life of capitalism itself would be endangered. Habermas, in his analysis of capitalism, asks for more than is needed from the state's crisis-avoidance scenario. It need do much less than he demands of it. In other words, the rationality deficit might not be as great as he thinks it is. But even if it were, there is still another way out short of the kind of planning that would violate advanced capitalism's boundary conditions – *arms expenditures*.

VII

Admittedly, the ability of the state to reduce its purposive-rational actions to the lowest level compatible with the continued legitimation of capitalism can certainly be disputed because it has never been adequately demonstrated. The first full-scale attempt was by the super-Keynesian economists under the Kennedy and Johnson administrations, but their 'fine-tuning' gamesmanship was quickly scuttled by the Vietnam War. The ability of advanced capitalism to ward off its inherent tendency toward chronic deflation can instead be most easily and most simply explained by the role of arms expenditures as the major prop of capitalist society. This, too, was foreseen by Luxemburg in her *Accumulation of Capital* and by Michal Kalecki.

Luxemburg's analysis in the brief last chapter of her book was inadequate. Although she linked arms expenditures to her theory of "external" markets, she did not fully appreciate their positive impact on capitalism's viability through their income-generating effects.[20] She failed to consider their financing via government deficits and their ability, therefore, to compensate in part for capitalism's need for external markets in order to 'realize' surplus value and maintain the rhythm of accumulation – though one could hardly have expected her to have seen the connection in 1913. Kalecki was much influenced by her arguments and saw the full import of arms expenditures for capitalist society. In his prophetic 1943 article, Kalecki argued that "one of the important functions of fascism, as typified by the Nazi system, was to remove the capitalist objections to full employment." Capitalist aversion to government spending was "overcome by concentrating Government expenditure on armaments." Writing twenty years later, in 1964, Kalecki added to his earlier argument.

> One of the basic functions of Nazism was to overcome the reluctance of big business to large scale government intervention. German big business agreed to a deviation from the principles of *laissez-faire* and to a radical increase of the role of government in the national economy.... However, the purely capitalist mode of production was guaranteed by directing the increased government expenditures to armaments *rather than to productive investment*....
>
> *Today government intervention has become an integral part of "reformed" capitalism.... Thus fascism is no longer the necessary basis of a system of government intervention.*[21]

Yet armaments continue to be a significant underpinning of advanced capitalist society. The preference for channeling government expenditures into armaments "rather than to productive investment" can be sensibly explained in terms of Domar's growth model. Contrary to popular opinion, the spinoff of arms expenditure technology to the private sector is much smaller than generally supposed.[22]

Moreover, armaments, as distinct from the production of investment goods, add nothing to the productive capacity of the economy. Government investment in armaments (A) involves an accumulation of capital goods that are in themselves barren – armaments are means of destruction, not means of production. Their average productivity (σ) is zero, unlike such other forms of government investment as urban transportation and education. Therefore, to the full extent that government investment is concentrated in armaments, $A\sigma = 0$; that is, it adds nothing to the productive capacity of the economy. But insofar as armament expenditures are financed through budgetary deficits, they do pump considerable purchasing power into the demand side. If the military supply multiplier is zero, the demand multiplier (k) is not. Therefore, Ak adds to effective demand and to that extent helps to resolve the basic dilemma of capitalism by furnishing the wherewithal to absorb the increased aggregate supply of private and nonarmament public investments that do add to the productive capacity of the economy. To that extent capitalism's reliance on 'external' markets, as Luxemburg argued, is significantly lessened, although by no means removed. Capitalism's ability to 'realize' its surplus value *internally* is far greater than even Luxemburg imagined. In effect, arms expenditures constitute an *internal-external* market. No wonder that capitalists prefer "directing increased government expenditures to armaments rather than to productive investment." The latter creates a problem, the former adds significantly to its solution.

Michal Kalecki's argument wedded to the Domar model might seem a bit exaggerated, if not hysterical. It would be useful, therefore, to look at the most recent data available.[23] Total worldwide military expenditures in 1975 (using constant 1973 dollars) were approximately $300 billion (American billion). Over a sixteen-year period, from 1960 to 1975, military expenditures in constant dollars rose by 78 percent from a base of $169 billion to an annual average of $244 billion. The United States and the Soviet Union account for 60 percent of world military expenditures and 80 percent of arms exports to other nations (50 percent for the United States and 30 percent for the USSR). The top six world powers (including West Germany, China, Britain, and France) account for 90 percent of world expenditures and the international trade in arms. The United States and NATO Europe account for roughly one-half the world total, whereas the USSR and the Warsaw Pact allies account for approximately 30 percent. Between them, the two blocs are responsible for 80 percent of total world military expenditures. The NATO countries of Europe spent $41 billion in 1973, compared to $8 billion by the Warsaw Pact (excluding the Soviet Union). The United States and the USSR spent

$79 billion and $67 billion, respectively, of the $244 billion world total for 1973.

From 1960 to 1975, the *cumulative* world total for the sixteen-year period (at 1976 prices) exceeded 4×10^{12} or 4 *trillion* dollars, with the stockpile of weapons worth $1 trillion, or twice the value of all the manufacturing fixed capital of the United States. In 1975, one-fifth of world military output, or $60 billion, was spent on nuclear weapons. By 1977, the two superpowers had five times more missile warheads than in 1969. The United States and the USSR stockpiles of such weapons add up to the equivalent of 1.3 million Hiroshima-size bombs. *With such data, the only conclusion any reasonably intelligent human being can possibly arrive at is that the genetic pool of mankind is irretrievably laced with insanity.*[24]

To continue this sad recital, one out of every four scientists in the world is involved in military 'defense' work, and of all public and private research and devlopment (R&D) expenditures in the world, 40 percent is committed to improving the arsenal. The United States and the USSR alone spend on the average between $20 and $23 billion (American billion) a year on military R&D, or about three-quarters of the world total. Most foreign aid to underdeveloped countries, moreover, is military in nature, with the major industrial countries exporting their obsolete equipment to them while replacing their own stockpiles with the latest technological improvements.[25] Throughout the world, 60 million people are either in the armed services or civilians working for the military establishment, with the various departments of defense exerting a profound political influence on their respective governments. Military budgets, as a result, have become sacrosanct – so much so that they have become impervious to the ups and downs of the economy.

In the United States, the defense budget, at $100 billion (American billion), is 25 percent of the federal budget and accounts for the direct and indirect employment of 7 million persons, or 7 percent of the total labor force. There is therefore a large vested interest in the arms industry, which receives approximately $40 billion a year for hardware and military R&D. Looking at the two superpowers of the world, the U.S. GNP (gross national product) is roughly twice as large as that of the USSR. To maintain parity, the USSR is therefore forced to spend 11 percent of its GNP on military expenditures, compared to 6 percent for the United States. This makes it tempting for the United States to use an accelerated arms race as a major Cold War weapon, by increasing military expenditures in order to force the USSR into financial and economic difficulties, thus increasing internal unrest by forcing a lower standard of living on the Soviet people.[26] But apart from this dangerous game and the international power politics involved, military expenditures do serve an important supportive function in capitalist economies. They add to effective purchasing power without increasing the productive capacity of the economy on the supply side.

Some researchers in the field argue that military expenditures slow down the rate of increase in the productive capacity and growth of a capitalist economy by siphoning off resources that could have been used in the private sector with greater effectiveness and efficiency. But this would be true if capitalism tended to operate consistently at a full employment level. If, on the contrary, advanced capitalism prefers to operate along the lines of Michal Kalecki's *political* theory of the trade cycle, with submerged peaks and the substitution of politically tolerable recessions for depressions that threaten the legitimation of capitalism, then arms expenditures are an important part of capitalist society. To argue that a cut in arms expenditures need not result in a severe economic downturn in view of such needed social expenditures as hospitals, mass urban transportation systems, and the like, is the capitalist equivalent of pushing numbers around "on uncomplaining paper." It is to fail to understand the internal dynamics of advanced capitalism. The problem is that 'on paper' budget deficits incurred for useful social projects could be used to solve the 'Keynesian' problem, but under the rules of the game they cannot be made as profitable for capitalist business as cuts in corporate income taxes, accelerated depreciation, and tax credits for new investment – all of which serve to increase the cash flow to the private sector with no guaranty that it will be used to bring the economy to its full employment level. Instead, capitalism's preference is to operate below its full potential in order to maintain the disciplinary effect of what Kalecki called the "fear of the sack." Except for a few occasional lapses, this is rarely admitted publicly. The rhetoric is usually in terms of the dangers of inflation.

The drive to accumulate capital, however, continues to be the driving force behind capitalism, but not at a rate that would threaten the vital interests of the capitalist class. Luxemburg was right. Capitalist accumulation *is* restrained, as Keynes himself was prepared to admit, but not only because of the profit-motive constraint. Habermas's "boundary conditions" are another element, though he tends to underestimate their flexibility under extraordinary conditions. It is only when the capitalist rate of accumulation is directly challenged from an external source that capitalism reacts at first sharply and then adapts its boundary conditions to the changed circumstances – a subject to which we now turn.

5

Beyond advanced unplanned capitalism

> There shall be wailing in every street,
> and in all open places cries of woe . . .
> there shall be lamentation in every vineyard . . .
> The day of the Lord is indeed darkness, not light,
> a day of gloom with no dawn.
>
>   – Amos

I

The constant refrain of Marxian and neo-Marxian analysis is that capital accumulation and growth are essential for the survival of capitalism. It was on this issue that the great debate broke out between Rosa Luxemburg and her critics. Growth was seen to be based not only on capital accumulation but also on technological change, which now serves as *the* major productive force of capitalism. If for any reason growth should not be possible, then capitalism would be faced with a deadly challenge leading ultimately to its destruction – or so it would seem on the basis of Marxian theory.

We should, however, step back and look at an earlier time when mercantilists were convinced that universal growth was an impossibility and acted accordingly. The strife and struggles of that time are relevant for the world of today, which is now entering its own phase of mercantilist power politics.

The earlier mercantilism of the seventeenth and eighteenth centuries emerged, out of the economic chaos of feudalism, as the builder of the great nation-states. Its greatest development came in France under Louis XIV (1638–1715) and his brilliant finance minister, Jean-Baptiste Colbert (1619–83). Mercantilists were acute observers of the world they lived in. Their primary concern was with power in a world of relentless political and economic warfare.[1] Power was to be consolidated in the state. The *Raison d'Etat* was far more important than the rights of individuals. Indeed, the welfare of individuals was dependent on that of the state, and it was the function of the state to guaranty the general welfare and hence the welfare of each indi-

71

vidual. The natural state of affairs among nations was one of conflict and war, and economic policy was shaped in that light. All internal activity was to be subservient to the interest of the state and closely controlled in a world continuously at war – from the end of the sixteenth century to the defeat of Napoleon in 1815. It was a matter of sheer survival.

There was no possibility for a peaceful expansion of all nation-states. It was ruled out by their static view of the world. The world's resources were regarded as being fixed. Consequently, one nation's gain implied another's loss. "The profit of one man," wrote Montaigne in 1580, "is the damage of another . . . no man profiteth but by the loss of others." Almost a century later, in 1669, Colbert laid out the argument coldly in realpolitik terms. "Trade," he wrote to Louis XIV, "causes perpetual strife in time of war and in time of peace between all nations of Europe to decide which of them shall have the greatest share." It was this static view of the economic universe that drove the mercantilists to pursue ruthlessly the game of power politics. "Any attempt," observed Heckscher, "at economic advance by one's own efforts in one country . . . appeared pointless, unless it consisted in robbing other countries of their possessions."

The more sophisticated mercantilists were even willing to suffer a diminution in their own welfare, provided that in so doing their enemies experienced an even greater decline. This *relative* gain in power was thought to be even more effective in promoting the welfare of one's own country in power terms.* In a world where all nation-states were simultaneously trying to obtain a larger slice of a given economic pie, conflict was the inevitable result. And although each nation came out worse in the immediate short run, a nation gained relatively if its losses and the attrition of its economy were less than that of its adversaries. All mercantilists, however, believed in a high level of domestic economic activity in order to provide an adequate tax base for a powerful state. Although static in its conception of the outside world, mercantilism was thoroughly dynamic in its domestic economic policies. It encouraged and helped found new industries through patents of monopoly, company charters, and outright subsidization.

It was out of this desperate and frightening view of the world and the mass of controls imposed on the economy and the individual that the radical liberalism of classical economics arose. In the new view,

---

*In modern terms: a preemptive strike based on nuclear superiority. A Harvard professor argued, in 1977, that the United States would get the better of a nuclear exchange with the USSR, and that nuclear war is not as unthinkable as others have argued. The 'balance of terror' has tilted, in his opinion.

private vice was automatically transformed into public virtue, not only without "the dextrous management of skillful politicians," but on condition that they would be prevented from exercising their dubious talents at all. An innate harmony of the universe was posited, based on John Locke's theories of natural rights and the rights of private property. The economic universe was no longer seen as finite. Through peaceful trade and the international division of labor, *all* nations could simultaneously increase their welfare. From 1870 to 1914, a period of almost half a century, peace reigned supreme and capitalism entered its great expansionary phase. All was right with the world as the Age of the Possible strode triumphantly onto the stage, with capital accumulation and growth firmly established on their single throne.

In 1798, well before capitalism got into its full stride in the latter part of the nineteenth century, the Reverend Malthus's apocalyptic theory of population cast a pall on the possibility of continual growth. Given the state of technology, the apocalypse was seen as a function of population and food. The former was subject to a geometric rate of growth, whereas the latter was subject to the 'law' of diminishing returns. As population grew in its exponential way, more and more land of decreasing fertility had to be brought under cultivation to feed it. Total output of food therefore increased at a *decreasing* rate. This was a catastrophe theory of the first order. If man could not bring his numbers under voluntary control, then nature would see to it through pestilence, starvation, and war. The 'laws' of nature could not be repealed; they could only be borne. Man transgressed them at his mortal peril. It was a 'no exit' situation. The counterattack was simple. Technology was *not* a constant. Through capitalist technology (and growth) the apocalypse was indefinitely put off. It was an un-mixed blessing that allowed the cornucopia of growth to disgorge an ever-increasing amount of goods.

These happy days were brought to an abrupt halt with the Great Depression of the 1930s and the resumption of neomercantilist beggar-thy-neighbor policies that led ultimately to World War II. It was enough to kill off the simplistic notions of liberal capitalism. The Keynesian Revolution proclaimed the end of laissez-faire and rein-troduced the role of government in the economy. Capitalism moved from its liberal to its advanced phase under a new set of boundary conditions. At first, a White Paper was written in England committing the government to maintaining 'full' employment and, more tellingly, the U.S. government, under the Employment Act of 1946, committed itself to the maintenance of the more ambiguous concept of 'maximum' employment. A new legitimation by all means, but at a

73

politically tolerable level of less-than-full employment. The Keynesian teeth had been pulled and its claws clipped. It had been tamed along the lines that Michal Kalecki foresaw. The postwar period saw the resumption of growth, with the inherent deflationary tendency of capitalism offset by the postwar conversion period, a Cold War, and two very hot Far Eastern wars. In the 1970s, as in the 1960s, with the stimulus of war gone, capitalism in its advanced stage sagged critically – though still within the politically tolerable limits described above. Then came two unexpected blows from two unexpected sources.

The first was a direct attack on technology. If technology at first pushed the Malthusian specter into the shadows, it now reemerged in the tattered regalia of a new apocalypse. It was technology itself that now threatened man with ecological disaster. It had become a powerful and arrogant force. In its conquest of nature, it displayed the conqueror's contempt for his victim. In response to technology's blundering transgressions, nature now threatens to exact a terrible revenge – a precipitous and irreversible descent into chaos. Yet apart from the ecological threat of technology, there is an even more immediate threat to man's physical existence. Technology has become dehumanized, with its most spectacular achievements dedicated to the total extermination of man. Because of a dehumanized and lunatic technology, mankind hovers on the brink of catastrophe. The brink, however, is round, and there are many approaches to the bottomless pit.

The most appalling of the lot would be a war in which atomic bombs were exchanged. *One* twenty-megaton bomb exploded 20 miles in the air would start with a fireball 4.5 miles wide that could ignite a man's clothing 21 miles away and produce retinal burns 340 miles away. The blast effect would be capable of picking up a man 15 miles from ground zero and smashing him into a wall. Pressure waves would create winds of more than 1,000 miles an hour quickly followed by massive firestorms. The destructive effect of a multibomb nuclear attack, moreover, would be greater than the sum of the individual bombs delivered. Deaths would be in the millions. In the case of enhanced-radiation neutron bombs, which destroy human life while leaving capital intact, the only human survivors would be those who, at the exact moment of detonation, happened to have been encased in paraffin or at the bottom of their dive into a deep swimming pool. All others would be dead after one or two days of extreme and agonizing pain. No wonder that Luis Buñuel had one of his characters exclaim in his film *The Milky Way:* "My hatred toward science and technology will surely drive me back to the despicable belief in God."

The second blow to the status quo of advanced, unplanned capitalism was the return to a mercantilist concept of a finite economic universe. Capital accumulation and growth could not go on forever and for everyone; resources were finite in supply. The consequences of mindless growth, even at restrained capitalist levels, would ultimately come up against an insurmountable wall. With computers now pushing the numbers around, catastrophe scenarios pinpointed the collapse at the end of the twentieth century or within the next 150 years at the latest. And this time technology could not, as in the past, come to the rescue. It, itself, and independently of the finiteness of the economic universe, was the problem. The imperatives of economic and technological growth in a finite economic universe spelled the doom of all modern industrial societies, regardless of the ideologies upon which they were based. Moreover, the finiteness of the world's resources was, as in Luxemburg's earlier theory of a finite world, a *theoretical* limit. The actual collapse of capitalism would come earlier, again as Luxemburg argued, with the major capitalist nations fighting among themselves for access to the increasingly limited stocks of raw materials essential for their survival – as indeed, during the heyday of the older mercantilism, the main combatants were the major countries of their time (Britain, France, Spain, and the Netherlands).

Advanced capitalism is now approaching, if it has not already reached, a neoimperialist and neomercantilist mode of operation that will, within a neo-Luxemburgist framework, strain capitalism's adaptability to its outermost limits. Unlike Luxemburg's catastrophe theory, however, capitalism's demise, should it come, will not be the result of internal contradictions, but rather the result of forces external to capitalism. In its successive transformations, capitalism has been able so far to avoid disaster by adapting itself to the forces of changing historical circumstances. But the new catastrophe theory interprets the entire historical metabolism of capitalism as a mad process of unremitting growth propelling it with increasing speed toward an 'objective' wall of exhausted resources – although the wall exists, as in Luxemburg, in the form of a theoretical wall with disruptive *political* forces in the forefront. The legitimation crisis of capitalism, in this context, is not a matter of an internal rationality deficit, as Habermas would have it, but more simply the revenge of a nature external to man.

The crisis also applies with equal and perhaps more strident force to a 'true' communist society insofar as it, too, would fail to adjust to the external constraints of nature. It would be a matter of pure speculation, and much beside the point, to argue that in its humaneness a true communist society would come to terms with nature rather than indulge in the futile insistence that nature come to terms with man's subjective desires. The fact remains that capitalism alone is faced with the actual choice, including for these purposes the Soviet Union as a capitalist system based on 'universal' private property.

II

The history of all capitalist growth and capital accumulation is the history of an extravagant use of the earth's resources. In 1975, for example, the capitalist countries of the West had 18 percent of the world's population and were only one-third as large as the population of all the underdeveloped countries. Yet they consumed 90 percent of nonferrous metals, 80 percent of petroleum and natural rubber, and 50 percent of raw cotton, vegetable oils, and sugar. From 1954 to 1970, the export prices of the developing countries, the major suppliers of raw materials, fell by 1 percent while their import prices rose by 12 percent. The net overall effect was a redistribution of the world's limited real resources from underdeveloped to capitalist countries, forcing a majority of the world's population to subsidize a very rich minority.

This was the way the system worked, in broad outline, until 1973, when a small group of underdeveloped countries sitting on top of the world's largest petroleum reserve reacted to the Middle East crisis by slapping an oil embargo on the capitalist countries of the West. By so doing, they threatened the energy base of capitalist society and therefore its ability to function at all. In terms of this crisis, the Marxist arguments of capitalism's fatal dependence on growth is not as far-fetched as it might seem. Indeed, the major capitalist country in the world was quick to agree to this basic Marxist proposition. In a speech before the World Energy Conference in Detroit on September 23, 1974, President Ford laid out the problem in stark mercantilist terms:

> Throughout history nations have gone to war over natural advantages, such as water or food, or convenient passages on land or sea. But in the nuclear age ... local conflict may escalate to global catastrophe. ... It is difficult to discuss the energy problem without lapsing into doomsday language. The danger is clear. It is severe.

The concerted action of the OPEC (Organization of Petroleum Exporting Countries) countries represented, in effect, a dry run of the ultimate catastrophe facing capitalism should economic growth no longer be possible and should it prove to be unable to adjust to the new circumstances. Speaking on the same day before the United Nations, the then secretary of state, Henry Kissinger, acknowledged the critical importance of growth and capital accumulation for the viability of advanced capitalism:

> The economic history of the postwar period has been one of sustained growth. . . . *The universal expectation of our peoples, the founding of our political institutions, and the assumption underlying the evolving structure of peace are all based on the belief that this growth will continue.* . . . [The] global economic system that we have come to take for granted is now under unprecedented attack. The world is poised on the brink of a return to unrestrained economic nationalism . . . [and] the collapse of economic order. . . . *The complex, fragile structure of global economic cooperation required to sustain national economic growth stands in danger of being shattered.*[2]

One can easily read into Kissinger's statement virtually all Habermas's arguments of a rationality crisis, externally imposed, that threatens the very legitimation of an advanced capitalism based on limitless accumulation and growth. One month later in a *New York Times* interview (October 13, 1974), Kissinger took the next step. Kissinger's "nightmare," as he described it, was that unless the interdependence of the major advanced capitalist countries was recognized and their actions coordinated in a true system of global planning to protect their access to the raw materials of the Third World,

> Western civilization . . . is most certain to disintegrate because it will first lead to a series of rivalries in which each region will try to maximize its own special advantages. That inevitably will lead to tests of strength of one sort or another. These will magnify domestic crises in many countries, and *they will move more and more to authoritarian models.* I would expect then that we will certainly have crises which no leadership is able to deal with [i.e., Habermas's rationality deficit], and probably military confrontations. But even if you don't have military confrontations, you will certainly, in my view, have *systemic crises* . . . under conditions when world consciousness has become global. [Italics supplied]

In a world where economic growth becomes the problematic, either because of natural or artificially induced limits, the world will enter a neomercantilist phase. In a static economic universe, Adam Smith's and John Stuart Mill's "stationary state" notwithstanding, the major preoccupation will be the political power of the nation-state. This was Kissinger's "nightmare," and it explains his repeated calls for an integration of policy among the leading capitalist countries of the world, and his fear, short of global planning, of the rise of economic nationalism, with the next phase of advanced capitalism one in which an *authoritarian* state solution will replace the unplanned character of contemporary capitalism.

As in mercantilist times, the economic life of a nation will be subordinated to the political ends of the state. Under extreme circumstances, power will be conceived in relative terms. The idea of power will be defined in terms of a country's economic potential in a world of finite resources. Any attempt to improve one nation's position absolutely will seem as pointless as it did to the mercantilists of the sixteenth and seventeenth centuries, "unless it consists in robbing other countries of part of their possessions." Bounded by a finite economic universe, dynamic means will be used *within* the state and the needed domestic regulation of the economy will lead to a total socialization of investment. The conundrum of independent investment markets, which served as the most important of the three factors adding up to the internal contradiction of advanced capitalism in Habermas's analysis, will be resolved by authoritarian means. The administrative technocrats will be in full control, with the 'steering mechanism' firmly in their hands. Foreign policy will also be dominated by the existence of a finite economic universe. With a fixed supply of world resources, the increased demand of the advanced countries (which increases more than in proportion to their increase in income) will lead to an increase in world prices. The price mechanism will price many poor countries out of the market, leading to a redistribution of scarce resources, even more unequally than before, to nations of greater wealth and power. The advanced capitalist countries will therefore need to control their Third World sources of supply politically and militarily. These Third World countries will become the disenfranchised lumpenproletariat of the world, dominated by indigenous military regimes and the controlling reactionary classes of client states.

But the authoritarian postcapitalist world envisioned by Kissinger will have its own system of legitimation. In one way or another, capitalism *will* adjust to changed circumstances and adapt its institutions accordingly, as it has in the entire history of its evolution. And it is this adaptability of capitalism that Habermas and other neo-Marxists fail to face up to in their search for internal contradictions. Indeed, the end of the dialectic may well come about not in a classless society, but in the fusion of science and ideology under an advanced

78

form of capitalism. Along these lines, Leo Strauss made a distinction between modern tyranny and classical tyranny that bears repeating:

> In contradistinction to classical tyranny, present-day tyranny has at its disposal "technology" as well as "ideologies"; more generally expressed, it presupposes the existence of "science," i.e., of a particular interpretation, or kind, of science. Conversely, classical tyranny, unlike modern tyranny, was confronted, actually or potentially, by a science which was not meant to be applied to "the conquest of nature" or to be popularized and diffused. . . .
>
> It is no accident that present-day political science has failed to grasp tyranny as what it really is. Our political science is haunted by the belief that "value judgments" are inadmissible in scientific considerations, and to call a regime tyrannical clearly amounts to pronouncing a "value judgment." . . . We are now brought face to face with a tyranny which holds out the threat of becoming, thanks to "the conquest of nature" and in particular human nature, what no earlier tyranny ever became: *perpetual and universal.* Confronted by the appalling alternative that man, or human thought, must be collectivized either by one stroke and without mercy or else by slow and gentle processes, we are forced to wonder how we could escape from this dilemma.[3]

Working together, political ideology and the empirico-analytical scientific paradigm will be engaged in the legitimation and consolidation of the new power structure. It will not be a jackbooted authoritarianism. Zbigniew Brzezinski, Kissinger's equivalent in the Carter administration, has already given us a peek into this brave new world.[4] His basic position is that the technetronic society of the future will be the result of the impact of technology and electronics on our social and cultural existence. It will be a manipulated society in which individual conduct will be less spontaneous in that it will be determined by and subject to deliberate programming. Economic power will be depersonalized in a complex, interdependent structure consisting of "governmental institutions (including the military), scientific establishments, and industrial organizations." Stability will be achieved in a totally controlled environment with domestic counterinsurgency programs inspired by and run by technetronic élite universities.

Brzezinski's revolution will be unlike all other revolutions of the past in that it will have "no charismatic leaders with strident doctrines." The end of ideology will be at hand, and running the technetronic society will be an élite meritocracy. For the rest, the masses, work will be converted into play, with a subtle, invisible regimentation of their leisure time. The legitimation of the new system will be based on a seeming transformation from an achievement- to a pleasure-oriented, "amusement-focussed" society under tightly controlled conditions, with "well-nigh total political surveillance" of every citizen. Universities will be for the qualified élite working in think-tank complexes serving the new technetronic leadership. There will be no 'formal' politics of the kind that Habermas talked about in describing advanced capitalism. Instead, we will have the emergence of the new mandarins – politician-intellectuals, who will fall into the categories of experts, specialists, and generalist-integrators.

The new version of a totally planned, postadvanced capitalism, however, will have the trappings of democracy. Through what has been called "the blueing of America," entry into the meritocratic élite will be strictly on the basis of natural ability, with meritocrats drawn from all socioeconomic classes. The new meritocratic society will therefore have the *semblance* of liberation, but it will be a liberation based on superior knowledge. In this sense, earlier forms of totalitarianism were before their time. They were, in large part, based on the coupling of evil with ignorance. The 'new' authoritarianism will be pleasure-oriented and benign, with a meritocratic élite at the helm ministering, efficiently, to the needs of the common man, albeit in a finite economic universe, or at least in one perceived to be so.

This is one possibility. Should it fail, capitalism will become openly polarized, legitimation will no longer be possible, and the answer will be a military solution such as the one described in the Kerner Commission report.[5] The polarization of the United States will be between core ghetto-cities consisting of blacks, Puerto Ricans, and the poor, and the ring of suburban middle-class communities surrounding them. As the predominantly white middle class flees to suburbia, it takes with it the political influence to allocate governmental resources for new schools, roads, fire departments, and other needed social services. Whatever resources are left will go to the core cities in the form of a retrained National Guard, riot control training for the police, and their provisioning with rubber bullets and armored vehicles – in short, a military solution that will not stop at political assassination, if needed (and as it was thought to have been in the case of the Black Panthers). The new authoritarianism will then be out in the open and dependent on raw power, with no pretense at legitimation.

These are two alternatives, neither of them palatable. There is also a third more complicated and perhaps more realistic alternative.

Capitalism's legitimation will be based on an appeal to 'interdependence', and on the domestic level it will seek to change advanced capitalism from an unplanned to a *planned* society in order to cope with the finiteness of the world's resources. The integration of the two approaches will serve to provide advanced capitalism with a new basis for legitimation under a new set of boundary conditions. The transition will not be a smooth one – less so on the international level, where it will be more difficult to integrate and subdue contending factions and conflicting interests.

The crisis of 1973–4 can be used as a case study of things to come and the paths of adaptation capitalism might follow as it approaches, in fact, the wall of finite resources in a neomercantilist world. It is useful, therefore, to analyze in greater detail these recent events and the reaction of the capitalist countries to the oil embargo.

III

Analytically, the new mercantilist world in the process of emerging can be broken down into three major blocs that share common ideologies or world views. They are the capitalist bloc, consisting of twenty-four countries; the eleven countries making up the communist bloc; and the over 100 countries making up the Third World or LDCs (Least Developed Countries). The use of the word 'bloc' does not imply a unanimity within any one bloc devoid of internal stresses and strains. Sharp differences exist, for example, between the Soviet Union and China, between the United States and France over the nature of the capitalist alliance, and between the OPEC countries and the non-oil-producing LDCs. In times of crisis, however, countries do tend to operate within their respective blocs despite internal differences.

The three-bloc model, moreover, is a useful way of looking at the distribution of population and world output and the power interrelationships that depend in an essential way not only on the distribution of world output, but also on the unequal distribution of the world's resources among them. All these relationships and their attendant institutional structures make up what can be called the International Economic Order (IEO). Each of the first two blocs is dominated by one of the two superpowers of the world: the United States and the Soviet Union. These are the two giants of our time, and they have one thing in common: *Giants have great stomping power* and are not afraid to use it, if they have to. The danger is that they may panic and use it precipitously if they sense a large-scale threat to their vital interests.

The entire postwar period was at first dominated by an East–West confrontation that resulted in the Cold War, with most of the LDCs solidly within the capitalist sphere of influence. While the East–West confrontation eased into détente, the Old International Economic Order (OIEO), which had worked so well for so long, was suddenly shattered in 1973 by a major North–South confrontation. The new confrontation was now between the capitalist and Third World blocs, with strident calls for the establishment of a New International Economic Order (NIEO) based on a more equitable distribution of the world's wealth. Before getting into the details of this new confrontation, it would be useful to look at the economic base of the three blocs and the relative distribution of economic power among them. The accompanying table provides, in summary form, the distribution of population and world output among the three blocs in 1975. It also gives the production of the two basic energy sources (crude petroleum and coal) and crude steel – three products essential to the operation of any modern industrial society – and the foreign trade of the three blocs.

The capitalist bloc, with 18 percent of the world's population, accounted, in 1975, for almost two-thirds of the world's total output and foreign trade. From within the bloc, the United States emerges as *the* major world power, with 5 percent of the world's population producing almost one-quarter of the Gross World Product (GWP). The communist bloc, on the other hand, with a third of the world's population, produced only 22 percent of GWP, with the Soviet Union even more dominant in its bloc with 57 percent of total communist output. The LDCs show up as the international proletariat. They make up almost one-half the world's 4 billion (American billion) population; yet, in 1975, they produced only 14 percent of GWP. They also imported higher percentages of their GNP than any other bloc, and as important suppliers of minerals and other raw materials tied in with growth in the capitalist bloc, their exports as a percentage of GNP were higher still. Finally, the capitalist bloc accounts for roughly two-thirds of world trade, with only a 12 percent participation by the communist bloc, and of the major superpowers, the United States dominates the world scene, with a GNP almost twice that of its closest rival, the Soviet Union.

Under the OIEO, the terms of trade greatly favored the capitalist countries, with the LDCs providing the needed raw materials at bargain-basement prices. In effect, the poorest one-half of the world's population subsidizes the richest 18 percent, and the meager economic aid that flows back to the LDCs does little to benefit the world's masses, most of it going into the pockets of an indigenous élite, who are also provided with the means for keeping their corrupt and co-opted regimes in power – through military aid and the training of their military officer class in American camps and their police in special counterinsurgency schools. The lid was firmly on, and though the East–West struggle flared up from time to time, the North–South basis of the OIEO worked tolerably well.

True, some serious problems arose in Algeria, the Suez, and the Congo, but most were minor ones having to do with the changing of the guard in a never-ending series of coups d'état. On occasion, to ward off a potentially serious situation, the United States would underwrite some of them, as in Guatemala and Chile or, under 'extreme provocation,' send in the Marines, as it did in the Dominican Republic. The OIEO, in other words, functioned under the aegis of a Pax Americana, but history works in strange, unaccommodating, and unanticipated ways.

In 1973, the bottom suddenly fell out in a way that threatened the very viability of capitalism by directly attacking its ability to sustain its long-term rate of growth and capital accumulation. It had nothing to do with the internal contradictions of capitalism or its supposed rationality deficit. It was an *externally* imposed threat to its life line – energy, without which the industrial base of advanced capitalism would collapse. The 1973 crisis is therefore important as a paradigm of the future. It can be taken as a *dry run,* or as an artificial model of what might well happen in the longer run in a world of truly finite resources. It is for that reason that particular attention will be paid to the oil crisis; especially to the reaction of the United States and the internal strains that were quick to appear within the capitalist bloc. The crisis of 1973, in short, can be used to shed some light on how capitalism might shift its 'boundary conditions' in order to cope with the catastrophe potential of a finite economic universe – through planning.

IV

In the winter of 1973–4, the Organization of Petroleum Exporting Countries (OPEC) announced a temporary oil embargo in retaliation against U.S. policy in the Middle East supporting Israel; although there is good evidence that the multinational oil cartel of the capitalist maneuvered behind the scenes to prod the OPEC countries into mbargo as a means for raising the price of oil dramatically. 'er the cause or the excuse, within one year the price of oil pled and double-digit inflation soon hit most advanced st countries. The immediate impact was to plunge the capitalist

1975 world population, output, production and foreign trade by blocs

Blocs	No. of countries	Population mid-1975 (millions)	GNP ($ U.S. billions)	Production (millions of metric tons)			Foreign trade ($ U.S. billions)			
				Crude petroleum	Coal	Crude Steel	Imports	Exports	Imports as % of GNP	Exports as % of GNP
Capitalist[a]	24	747	4,005	531	1,016	381	592	571	15	14
United States	1	214	1,516	413	581	106	97	108	6	7
Other	23	533	2,489	118	435	275	495	463	20	20
Communist[b]	11	1,329	1,389	593	1,389	221	108	93	8	7
USSR	1	255	787	491	566	141	37	33	5	4
Other	10	1,074	602	102	823	80	71	60	12	10
Rest of world (LDCs)	100	2,004	889	1,513	187	39	199	213	22	24
World total		4,080	6,283	2,637	2,592	641	899	877	14	14

1975 world population, output, production and foreign trade by blocs (cont.)

Blocs	No. of countries	Population mid-1975 (millions)	GNP ($ U.S. billions)	Production (millions of metric tons)			Foreign trade ($ U.S. billions)			
				Crude petroleum	Coal	Crude Steel	Imports	Exports	Imports as % of GNP	Exports as % of GNP
Percentages of world total										
Capitalist[a]	24	18	64	20	39	59	66	65		
United States	1	5	24	16	22	16	11	12		
Other	23	13	40	4	17	43	55	53		
Communist[b]	11	33	22	23	54	35	12	11		
USSR	1	6	12	19	22	22	4	4		
Other	10	27	10	4	32	13	8	7		
Rest of world (LDCs)		49	14	57	7	6	22	24		
World total	100	100	100	100	100	100	100	100		
Percentages within respective blocs										
United States		29	38	78	57	28	16	19		
USSR		19	57	83	41	64	34	56		
Combined % of world total		11	37	34	44	39	15	16		

[a]_Capitalist bloc countries:_ U.S., Canada, Japan, Australia, New Zealand, and the 19 OECD countries.
[b]_Communist bloc countries:_ USSR, Albania, Bulgaria, China, Cuba, Czechoslovakia, East Germany, Hungary, Poland, Rumania, and Yugoslavia.
Source: "Indicators of Comparative East-West Economic Strength, 1975," Department of State, Special Report No. 27, November 1976.

bloc into the most severe depression since the 1930s. Unemployment topped 15 million, half of which was in the United States. The oil price increase continued its heavy toll. The oil import bill for the capitalist bloc rose from $35 billion (American billion) in 1973 to $140 billion in 1977. Hardest hit, however, were the non-oil-producing LDCs. Their higher import bill for oil totally wiped out their receipts of foreign aid, and their debt service on borrowing, mostly from private bank sources, almost doubled within a few years. The European capitalist countries and Japan were in a far more critical position than the United States. The ensuing depression had a greater impact on them, given their greater dependence on external markets for their goods, not to mention their almost total dependence on imported oil. The United States, as head of the capitalist bloc, was quickly faced with the problem of holding the capitalist countries in line.

The initial reaction to the oil embargo was one of panic. Thinly disguised warnings of direct military action were made, as we have already seen, by the president and secretary of state. On January 13, 1975, Kissinger made the warnings even more explicit in his famous "strangulation" statement in an interview with *Newsweek*. In a television interview a few days later, he said he was only talking "hypothetically," but he repeated that though "military action is totally inappropriate . . . no nation can announce that it will let itself be strangled without reacting. . . . The United States will not permit itself or its allies to be strangled. Somebody else would have to make the first move. . . . There would have to be an overt move of an extremely drastic, dramatic, and aggressive nature before this contingency could be considered." The warning had been made, but even before the warning stories were leaked in 1974, shortly after the embargo, that the Department of Defense was engaged in long-range studies and contingency plans for the nine crucial "strategic checkpoints or maritime bottlenecks through which raw materials will flow . . . which we must dominate politically and militarily."[6]

The problem, however, was not "strangulation," but the undermining of capitalist legitimation based on growth and endless capital accumulation. Kissinger apparently was very much aware of the real nature of the challenge. "Our security, our economic growth, our role in the world are at risk," he announced. "Energy is at the heart of our industrial system." It was of paramount importance that "sustained and stable economic growth" be restored, because it is *so essential to maintain confidence in [our] institutions. . . .* Stagnation magnifies all our difficulties; stable growth enhances our possibilities." There was, furthermore, an imperative need "to encourage research and development necessary to advance *the technology vital to our growth.*"[7] The crisis was clearly seen as a full-blown *legitimation crisis,* as Kissinger admitted in neo-Marxian terms:

> Politically, as well as economically, our era has been shaped by the Industrial Revolution and the progress and economic growth that it brought. *At home, this economic progress has been an essential underpinning of our democracy. It is the basis of a stable, progressive, and just political environment.*

But the legitimation crisis was not purely an internal problem confined to legitimation "at home." It was a worldwide legitimation crisis involving the OIEO, because the growth of the capitalist bloc was essential for the international depoliticization of the distribution of the world's social product between the capitalist and Third World blocs. Without capitalist growth, the co-optation of the wealthy class in the underdeveloped countries would be impossible and the distribution of world output under the OIEO would be dangerously repoliticized, leading to an international class struggle between the 'haves' and 'have-nots'. Without growth, aid programs could not be continued, nor could expanding markets for LDC exports be maintained. As Kissinger acknowledged, only capitalist economic growth could satisfy the demand of LDCs for more income. When capitalist economies stagnate, there is an increase in "domestic and international pressures over the distribution of economic benefit." Capitalism was therefore caught up in a double legitimation bind: the repoliticization of distribution "at home" as well as abroad.

The OPEC problem was significantly eased, though by no means resolved, through the recycling and absorption of petrodollars into the capitalist economies. Direct and portfolio investment gave the OPEC cartel an increased stake in the United States and other capitalist economies. If Western capitalism was hostage to OPEC, OPEC soon became hostage to capitalism. The economic links between the capitalist bloc and OPEC became even tighter in the aftermath of the oil embargo, as OPEC purchased vast amounts of technology, machinery, spare parts, and military equipment from the West. OPEC had been effectively separated from the great majority of LDCs and co-opted into the capitalist sector.[8] Another unexpected side effect of the oil crisis was that the United States emerged in a stronger position than before. Its domination of the capitalist bloc was enhanced, given the greater vulnerability of the other capitalist countries and their greater dependence on imported oil. And it tied the capitalist nations even closer to itself by reversing détente and moving into a new, though somewhat milder, Cold War confrontation with the Soviet Union by 1977.[9]

V

The co-optation of the OPEC cartel still left a large segment of discontented non-oil-producing LDCs to contend with. The lessons of oil cartelization were not lost on the non-OPEC LDCs. There was more to capitalist vulnerability than its dependence on oil. There was the matter of minerals and other vital raw materials, independent of oil, without which capitalist growth would also not be possible. Within short order, the capitalist bloc was faced with a second confrontation in the wake of the OPEC 'holdup'. Luis Echeverria, the president of Mexico at the time, called for the imposition of "19th century trade union tactics" against the capitalist bloc. He called for the unification of raw-material countries into non-OPEC LDC cartels to exact higher prices and thereby redistribute world output more favorably toward the vast majority of the world's exploited population. The United Nations representative of Peru, Carlos Alzamora, rejected the OIEO as being based on "the power of those who impose" it.

The reaction of the capitalist bloc to this new challenge was more measured and less given to panic than had been the case in the oil crisis. The capitalist bloc more calmly assessed its power in relation to that of the non-OPEC LDCs. It promulgated the 'trickle-down theory' of capitalist economic growth and the dependence of the undeveloped countries on its continuance. The United States at first blustered a bit, then quickly reminded the LDCs of their dependence on the capitalist bloc. The blustering took the form of a series of pronunciamentos. "We shall resist the tactic of bloc confrontation." In any test of strength, "it is not the advanced industrial powers who will pay the highest price . . . it will be the poorest and the most disadvantaged – those in whose name and for whose benefit these tactics are purportedly used." The mercantilist theory of relative power was explicitly stated by Kissinger: "The industrial democracies [i.e., the capitalist bloc], as the wealthiest and most technically advanced, would best survive economic conflict." The LDCs, furthermore, "are not a natural bloc." Made up of over 100 countries differing widely in income and economic structure, their attempts to radicalize the Third World into an antagonistic and unified bloc were doomed to failure. Hotheads urged a 'spoilers' role' on the LDCs, but cooler ones judged the situation more accurately. As Kissinger testified before the Senate Finance Committee on January 30, 1976:

[T]he United States is the world's most powerful economy. Together with our allies among the industrial democracies, *we are the engine of global prosperity,* technological innovation and the best hope for widening economic opportunity to millions around the globe. *We could withstand an era of international economic warfare better than any.*

And in his speech to the Seventh Special Session of the United Nations, with over 100 LDCs gathered there to hammer out a redistribution of world income in a New International Economic Order (NIEO), Kissinger laid his cards on the table:

[T]he econoimc health of the industrial countries is central to the health of the global economy.... Development is a process of growth ... requiring the infusion of capital technology, and managerial skills *on a massive scale.*

And, of course, the capitalist bloc had a virtual monopoly over the high technology needed and the capital markets through which it had to flow on its way to the LDCs. Moreover, "80 percent of LDCs' foreign exchange earnings come from exports, mostly to advanced nations, and their annual growth rates are thus highly correlated with growth in rich countries." Kissinger issued a stern warning to the LDCs in his 1975 testimony before the Senate Foreign Affairs Committee. He announced a systematic effort on the part of the United States

to insure that each developing country understands that our bilateral relations with it include that country's behavior towards us in international meetings and, in particular, its votes on issues of the highest importance to us. I have asked each of our embassies overseas to make clear to its host government that one of the factors by which we will measure the value which the government attaches to its relations with us will be its statements and votes on that fairly limited number of issues which we indicate are more important to us in international forums.... [T]he United States will be weighing this factor more heavily in making new commitments within bilateral relationships.

On February 4, 1976, the secretary of state let the LDCs know upon whom they would have to count for their betterment:

Our technological advance, our managerial skills, our achievements in science and medicine, the productivity of our farms and industry, our physical resources ... – insure for us

> a role of leadership . . . [N]o other free [i.e., capitalist] nation is
> strong enough to replace us.

But it was not just science and technology that capitalism had to
offer as a reward for 'good' behavior. It also had a deadly and devastating power in what it could withhold. LDCs could survive without
advanced technology, no matter how much they needed and wanted
it, but they could not survive without food. The United States had the
retaliatory weapon of food power to offset petropower or raw-
material power. The world's total food requirement continued to increase. If the current gap between demand and supply was 25 million
tons of food, by 1985 it would reach 50 to 75 million tons. Moreover,
the ability of LDCs to expand their own food production was compromised by the scarce and increasingly expensive supply of
petroleum-based fertilizers. The "stark reality" was that in twenty-
five years there would be twice as many people to feed in the world,
especially in the LDCs with their "out-of-control" population growth
rates. Food was more than a critical need: It was a question of life and
death, with the United States providing 60 percent of all food aid on a
worldwide basis. From one-quarter to one-third of U.S. agricultural
land was geared to the food export market.

On top of this, Kissinger announced a "maximum food production"
policy for the United States and added menacingly that "we wish
cooperative relations with nations that purchase from us." If the
United States was experiencing an increasing dependency on LDCs
for vital minerals and raw materials, it was also the case that LDCs
were experiencing a higher and more critical dependency on the
United States for food – especially in view of dire long-run predictions
of a "permanent" world famine – and for technology. As Kissinger
pointed out, in any confrontation between the capitalist and LDC
blocs, it would not be the former that would suffer most.[10]

With a great deal of hoopla, the LDCs got together to set up the
NIEO in the Special Seventh Session of the United Nations (September 1–16, 1975). Kissinger's opening address laid down the hard
line. The message, however, had long since gotten through. The
LDCs demanded indexation and higher prices for their raw materials; they got instead an export-earning stabilization scheme to tide
them over hard times when world prices for their exports were low. It
was to be arranged through special borrowings from the International Monetary Fund, the World Bank, and other specialized international agencies – all under the control of the capitalist bloc and of the
United States in particular – and easier LDC access to capital markets,

provided, of course, that they behaved as they were expected to behave.

The LDCs demanded debt forgiveness and increased direct aid; they instead got promises of technical assistance and greater access to *private* capital markets. They asked for aid and instead got loans. They asked for increased direct foreign investment by the capitalist bloc and were told to rely on private capital flows and multinational corporations (MNCs) for their development – provided they stopped their harassment of MNCs and improved the private investment climate within their countries. The LDCs threatened to close off access to raw materials and instead were given "a comprehensive program of investment to expand worldwide capacity in minerals and other raw materials . . . basic to the health of both industrial and developing economies" – to be overseen by the U.S.-controlled World Bank, whose primary function would be to "use their technical, managerial, and financial expertise to bring together funds from private and public sources . . . [and to] *act as intermediary between private investors and host governments.*"[11]

The NIEO turned out to be the OIEO with a few concessions thrown in. Kissinger correctly assessed the situation. It was necessary "to encourage the developing nations to look at the real [neomercantilist] world, not the rhetorical world." In the meantime, it was also necessary to solidify the capitalist bloc under the leadership and domination of the United States, and to develop contingency and counterinsurgency plans should things get out of control. Proposals were made for a "'distant early warning' economic intelligence system, to alert [the capitalist bloc] to the stresses in the emerging global economic system *so problems can be prevented from becoming panics,*" as well as "'cross-sector' analysis of interdependence issues . . . *for anticipating crises and insuring that the foreign policy system is better organized for the long pull.*" It was even suggested that the State Department be reorganized "from a country desk basis to functional groups such as steel and energy."[12] More to the immediate point, an eighteen-member International Energy Association (IEA) was set up to develop the technology for alternate energy sources and to initiate a stockpiling program.[13]

The raw politics and pressure of the capitalist bloc were masked by a rhetoric of their own. Suddenly, a new slogan appeared on the scene: *Interdependence.* Its most extreme expression was given by Hans-Dietrich Genscher, the foreign minister of West Germany, in his September 24, 1975, speech to the Thirtieth Session of the United Nations General Assembly (italics supplied):

The irresistible trend towards ever greater interdependence is the distinguishing feature of the new age; it is the course of world history. For the first time mankind as a whole is moving towards a common future: either to survive together or to perish together, to prosper or to decline together. The world as a whole lives under *the iron law of interdependence*.... The growth rates of national economies have become interdependent.... *Higher growth rates in the industrialized countries mean higher growth rates in the developing countries, and lower growth rates in the industrialized countries mean lower growth rates in the developing countries.*

Two days earlier, before the same session of the General Assembly, Kissinger announced that "our interdependence spells either common progress or common disaster." "Peace," he went on to add, "is inseparable from security," and the security of the capitalist bloc was intimately tied to its access to raw materials "at reasonable prices" – as was the rate of growth and the very *legitimation* of the capitalist system. At the end of the Seventh Special Session of the United Nations, the U.S. representative of the Ad Hoc Committee of the Special Session, Ambassador Jacob M. Myerson, stated that "The United States cannot and does not accept any implication that the world is now embarked on the establishment of something called *the* 'new international economic order'" (italics supplied). There was, of course, no objection to *an* NIEO, provided it involved a minimally revised OIEO just sufficient to defuse a dangerous situation at the smallest possible cost to the capitalist bloc. The giant stomping power of the United States, poised threateningly in midair, had turned the trick, for the moment. The greatest surprise of all was that the United States had emerged from the unexpected crisis brought on by OPEC and the other LDCs with even greater power than before. It had successfully separated the OPEC cartel from the non-oil-producing LDCs and had bound the members of its own bloc more closely to itself, promulgating at the same time the 'interdependence' theme that in its asymmetry linked the fate of the non-OPEC LDCs to the rate of capital accumulation of the capitalist bloc. Global planning to assure access to raw materials was to be run by the major capitalist nations of the world in their own interest with a somewhat greater sensitivity to the needs of the poorer countries, though not enough sensitivity to threaten the vital economic interests of the countries dominant in the capitalist bloc.

A new form of mercantilism had emerged wrapped up in the raiment of 'interdependence', a trickle-down theory of capitalist growth, and the necessity for 'global planning'. The international 'boundary conditions' of advanced capitalism had shifted, but to the minimum extent necessary.

VI

The artificially induced crisis of 1973-7, artificial in the sense that it was not based on 'objective' conditions, is useful as a model for the coming struggles in a finite economic universe where resources are being ravenously depleted by the enormous consuming engine of economic growth. In the longer run, by the end of the century, the institutions of capitalism will have to be more radically transformed as capitalism approaches the wall of finite resources. A new international and domestic economic order is inescapable. As the Club of Rome concluded at its 1976 Philadelphia conference, in terms reminiscent of Rosa Luxemburg:

> In the conditions of the coming times, a viable world balance
> between population and resources – if the present generation
> is not able to timely adopt the necessary corrective measures –
> will inevitably tend to bring about *a technocratic version of
> Oriental despotism,* of which Stalinism and Nazism have already
> given us an anticipated view.[14]

We are back once more to Kissinger's "nightmare" of authoritarianism and Brzezinski's "enlightened" fascist vision of a meritocratic society. The nightmare, however, has a domestic as well as an international dimension. Large changes in the boundary conditions of capitalism will be necessary to adapt it to a world where growth, as it has been known in the past, is no longer possible. The 1973-7 international crisis was a *political* threat to growth that the capitalist bloc was able to overcome while holding together in the face of the most serious challenge to its existence in recent times. The problem now is whether capitalism will be able to hold together in the face of an 'objective' limit to economic growth which, if it in fact exists, could quickly involve the entire world in a mad scramble for increasingly scarce resources leading, as Luxemburg foresaw, to neoimperialist wars and a descent into barbarism.

Capitalism has shown over the course of its entire history a remarkable ability to adapt to changing circumstances and is already beginning to show a similar, though somewhat strained, flexibility in adapting to its biggest challenge of all – effective domestic planning in a finite mercantilist world of increasingly limited resources. Already, new forces are marshaling and preparing the way for the transition from an unplanned advanced capitalism to a planned postcapitalist state. At the 1975 meetings of the American Economic Association, a group of economists assembled to have a "serious" interchange on national economic planning.[15] It turned out to be a vapid discussion among a handful of preening academics more intent on scoring debating points than addressing the real issues. Its only importance, if any, was the willingness of the profession to raise the issue of systematic planning at all. It was, moreover, a shallow response to the discussions going on in the real corridors of power.

Congressional preparations were well under way, by 1975, to push U.S. capitalism toward a new form of economic planning. The institutional machinery of the Employment Act of 1946 became a sham and the Council of Economic Advisors, set up by the act, a political fraud. New bills were introduced in the Senate to reform the system and set up a form of national economic planning. After going through a series of revisions, Senator Hubert Humphrey submitted his Full Employment and Balanced Growth Act of 1976. In it, he expressed his concern over the "fundamental long-term problems *which seriously threaten the strength and vitality* of our capitalist system" (italics supplied). Indeed, he thought it to be in a state of crisis. New institutional structures were proposed to meet the crisis and to coordinate government policies on all levels and on a regional basis as well. Above all, it called for long-range economic planning. Only a decade or so ago, such a proposal would have been denounced as socialist by most of those now proposing it. Even so, it is a mild document consisting of a few minor adjustments to the Employment Act of 1946.

The proposed act substituted for the Council of Economic Advisors a much blown-up National Planning Agency, whose main business would be to accelerate the rate of growth of the world's most powerful capitalist nation. Its first objective would be to increase the flow of basic information upon which the needed 'planning' would be based. Given this qualitatively improved data base, an Economic Planning Board attached to the Executive Office of the President would devise not a single plan but a series of economic growth plans. A Council of Economic Planning, including Cabinet members, and an Advisory Committee of business, labor, and public representatives (appointed by the president and Congress) would send an agreed-upon plan to the Joint Economic Committee of Congress for hearings. The revised plan would then go to the Congress as a whole, where further changes would no doubt be made, and ultimately to the president for final approval and implementation.

As envisaged by Robert Heilbroner,

> [T]he planning process [will] closely resemble the legislative
> process . . . – there will be a struggle to insinuate many views.
> Corporate élites, charismatic individuals, powerful politicians,
> labor unions, regional and other lobbies, public groups of
> many sorts will be writing letters, taking people out to lunch
> or trying to pull strings to get some portion of the plan to
> represent their interests or points of view. . . . [The whole
> process] will . . . reflect the untidy, adversary, influence
> peddling ways by which a democratic system works.[16]

Heilbroner's vision is the consensus-forming, co-opting, *pluralist
paradigm* of capitalist democracy humming away in a sweet harmony
of reconciled differences – exactly what Habermas described as the
legitimating basis of advanced, *unplanned* capitalism. Under the new
regime, however, there will be some semblance of planning within the
same co-opting pluralist paradigm. Heilbroner has no fear that the
planning process will be captured by big business with the acquies-
cence of big government. Labor and consumer groups will see to that!
His faith in *consensus liberalism* is touching, if not naive. The fact
remains, however, that for the first time some form of 'planning' is
being discussed in response to a perceived, although vaguely de-
lineated, crisis in advanced capitalism. Yet the 'planning process' will
not be planning in the real sense. The various planning plans will
simply be improved crisis-avoidance scenarios, which will probably be
as ineffective in the end as were earlier attempts to fine tune the
economy to full employment along an optimal growth path.

But Heilbroner's darker side at times surfaces to give us another
view of planning's possible development: "If the plan is of the highest
importance for national survival," it will undoubtedly turn coercive.
But the coerciveness will consist of allocation priorities, direct aid for
certain types of investment, and other tamperings with the market
system, as in times of major wars and on the basis of a popular consensus based on a commonly perceived threat. But there is a still darker
side to Heilbroner: "The process of economic growth continues its
ravenous progress, reaching further and further into the earth's crust
for the materials essential for its continuance," with the exhaustion of
the more easily reached resources coming within a single generation.
Planning, in that eventuality, will become even more imperative and
more coercive, although Heilbroner balks at describing this more
ominous possibility. Others do not. Robert V. Roosa of Brown
Brothers Harriman, along with such industrialists and financiers as
Felix Rohatyn of Lazard Frères, Henry Ford, and David Rockefeller,

95

are apparently thinking along lines other than Heilbroner's comfortably 'democratic' pluralist paradigm. In a neomercantilist world of increasingly scarce raw material resources, the transition will most probably be to the state capitalist planning system geared to the international struggle for access to raw materials.

The Humphrey proposal, in any event, has been gutted to the shell of what it once was – a liberal's well-intentioned attempt to do something about a problem clearly seen but not squarely faced. A more hardheaded, realpolitik approach is that of the Trilateral Commission set up in 1973 by David Rockefeller, with the able assistance of the ubiquitous Zbigniew Brzezinski.[17] Membership in the commission, as in the Club of Rome, is international and consists of the world's most powerful bankers, multinational corporate executives, and government functionaries. Its main theme, not surprisingly, is 'interdependence', the need for global planning, and the domination and integration of the Third World by the capitalist bloc. Its task force reports, written largely by kept academics, emphasize the need for 'free trade' in a transnational world economy.

VII

The 1973 oil crisis and its aftermath can be seen as a preview of coming events. The increasing scarcity of energy and raw materials could well result in extremely low growth rates and a chronic global depression with massive unemployment in capitalist countries coupled with severe inflation. The impact on non-OPEC LDCs will be even more disastrous, regardless of higher raw material prices, given their population growth rates and the dependence of their export earnings on trade with a *growing* capitalist bloc. The legitimation crisis would be international as well as domestic. With even negative growth rates possible, the distribution of world and national outputs would be repoliticized in a world of turmoil and class struggle. In this kind of universe, the capitalist bloc could either splinter and fly apart or become completely subordinated to the major capitalist bloc country, the United States.

Brzezinski's meritocratic system could easily form the basis for the transition to a *planned* version of advanced capitalism dominated by a select group of industrialists and financiers with their high-powered technocrats firmly in tow. The boundary conditions of advanced capitalism will then have once more changed, only this time without the pretense of pluralist democracy. The legitimation of capitalism would be based on a technocratic control of society to cope with an international scene in turmoil. Like the 1930s *synarchiste* movement in

France, new and more effective Jean Coutrots would appear[18] calling for economic and social changes, while simultaneously rejecting unplanned capitalism as well as all forms of socialist planning. Liberalism and parliamentarianism would go by the boards. The new technocrats, à la Brzezinski, would replace intellectuals and fuzzy-headed politicians trying to rewrite the Employment Act of 1946. They would be the modern counterparts and products of the new ENAs, Ecoles Polytechniques, Ecoles Normales, and Ecoles des Sciences Politiques. In a word, Brzezinski's superélite universities – Kissinger's nightmare at last come true. Planned capitalist society's legitimation would be achieved via media control, surveillance, and a co-optation of the masses through a growth based on the predatory exploitation of weaker nations held firmly under political and military control – the 1973–7 scenario replayed with a vengeance.[19]

The descent into barbarism that Luxemburg so feared could become a reality in a world in which capital accumulation will be severely limited. But the 'barbarism' Luxemburg foresaw as a possibility not to be automatically ruled out by a mechanical dialectic will most probably not entail the 'catastrophic' collapse of capitalism but rather its dialectical transformation into an advanced, planned technocratic capitalism operating within newly defined boundary conditions.

Whether it will be a "technocratic version of Oriental despotism," or a form of benign totalitarianism based on *differentiated* growth, as the Club of Rome would have it, can only be a matter of conjecture. But whether either will come to pass is also a matter of pure speculation. Scenarios are just another form of pushing numbers around and are no better than the Marxian variety of number pushing. History has never turned out as expected, and the dream of a more perfect, more humane world continues unabated.

6

Beyond capitalism?

Yes, when the whole world from Paris to China
O godlike Saint-Simon, has accepted your teachings,
The golden age will return in all its splendor,
The rivers will run cocoa, tea,
Sheep will gambol ready roasted in the fields
Poached fish will swim in the Seine
Spinach will grow pre-fricasseed
With breadcrumbs all around
The trees will bear stewed apples
We will harvest vegetables by the bunch
It will snow wine, rain chicken
Ducks will fall from heaven à l'orange.
                              – Lauglé and Vanderbusch
                              Louis et le Saint-Simonien (1832)

I

Man has always dreamed of utopian societies and, in a few instances, all of which failed, has even tried to implement these dreams in experimental societies. Despite Marx's denunciation of utopian socialism, there was nevertheless a utopian strain in his thinking, as demonstrated in his 1844 *Paris Manuscripts*. Utopianism, however, is not limited to socialist or Marxian schemas. In a real sense, the pure theory of competitive capitalism is the biggest utopian dream of them all.

Modern socialism, moreover, at least in the West, bases its ultimate hope for liberation on the technology pioneered by liberal and advanced capitalist societies. Early Russian anarchists, of course, would have none of this. They were "Believers without God, Heroes without phrases," ever-prepared to leapfrog the dialectic into utopia. Even among confirmed Marxists there were those who, like Lenin and even Rosa Luxemburg, were at bottom hardheaded pragmatists quite prepared to trim their Marxian sails when the revolutionary potential suddenly and unexpectedly became a reality. They engaged in their own leapfrogging, much to the consternation of the Plekhanovs and

Kautskys who, as staunch guardians of Marxian orthodoxy, opposed the October Revolution as premature and therefore doomed to die.

The debate is now academic in the West. Capitalism has evolved into its advanced form with a massive technology at its base. But the dream of a 'true' revolution lingers on and is seen to be possible, for the first time in human history, only because of the advanced technology of modern capitalism. Herbert Marcuse's dream of the 'true' revolution[1] involved a Kuhnian paradigm shift from the current historical 'reality principle', which he labeled the "performance principle," to one that reconciles the pleasure and the reality principles in a polymorphously perverse society in which all labor is liberated and unalienated. Although every revolution in the past has been a betrayed revolution, Marcuse felt that for the first time in history the 'true' revolution was a real possibility – a revolution that would once and for all close the yawning gap between society's actual performance and its great potentiality. But the 'true' revolution has become possible only as a result of the enormous technological achievements of contemporary capitalism.

> If the completion of the technological project involves a break with the prevailing technological rationality, the break in turn depends on the continued existence of the technical base itself. For it is this base which has rendered possible the satisfaction of needs and the reduction of toil – *it remains the very base of all forms of human freedom.*[2]

The 'realm of necessity' in Marx's *Grundrisse* precluded man's liberation from all work. It is the basic ontological condition for all of human existence in a world of *Ananke* (the Realm of Necessity). Although man's burden can be progressively lightened through technology, it cannot be completely done away with. There is, in Marcuse's terms, a "basic repression" that, with the progress of science, declines asymptotically to a minimum level. But the technological rationality of capitalism superimposes upon this basic and unavoidable repression an increasing amount of "surplus repression," which more than swamps the fall in basic repression. *Total* repression in capitalist society therefore increases as it marches through historical time. Yet capitalism's development of high technology provides *the* basis for a utopia in which all surplus repression disappears. It is no longer a romantic dream, for Marcuse, but a practical possibility. For the first time, it is within man's reach and for the taking. Capitalism had the potential for true liberation but, in its turbulent historical development, failed; it became a deformed revolution. The attempt to apply Marxian principles to a technologically based society also failed in the

Soviet Union; it degenerated into a 'new' capitalist society of alienated labor based on massive repression. We are faced, then, with *two* deformed revolutions, both founded on the technological achievements of capitalism – with the 'true' revolution as far away as ever.

II

The major arguments presented so far can be summarized in the form of a set of diagrams based on Marcuse's notion of surplus repression and on Habermas's schema of traditional and capitalist societies. The vertical axis in all three diagrams measures total repression, which consists of the sum of basic and surplus repression ($R_T = R_B + R_S$). Basic repression is a decreasing function of science and technology, which starts at t_1 with the onset of the Industrial Revolution, and is asymptotic to the 'Realm of Necessity'. Historical time is on the horizontal axis. Human society cannot reach a level of zero repression except in death, which is represented by the 'Apocalypse' at the origin (A_0), where historical time is also annihilated, for history is simply an attribute of human existence.

In precapitalist, traditional society repression is shown as a horizontal line; it does not increase over time because surplus repression is assumed to be a constant. It is only with the onset of capitalism at t_1 that total repression increases, while at the same time basic repression declines with the application of technology to the production process. The distance between the R_T and R_B curves represents surplus repression (R_S), which increases as a function of historical time – at an increasing rate. Surplus repression, in other words, accelerates with the emergence of advanced capitalism in its unplanned phase until it reaches the point of self-destruction (A_{t_n}) in the upper lefthand diagram. For convenience, this can be equated with the culmination of the 'rationality deficit' of an *unplanned* advanced capitalist society (Habermas), which is unable to stretch its boundary conditions to accommodate itself to the changed circumstances of its historical existence. Alternatively, it can be equated with Luxemburg's *theoretical* breakdown (catastrophe) point. When capitalism has spread to all corners of the earth and has absorbed existing precapitalist enclaves internationally as well as domestically, capital accumulation is no longer possible because of the disappearance of external markets. Capitalism must therefore collapse out of 'objective' necessity. But as Luxemburg argued in her theory of imperialism, the collapse would come *before* the theoretical limit to capital accumulation would be reached, in the upper righthand diagram, at t_{n-1}. At this point, two

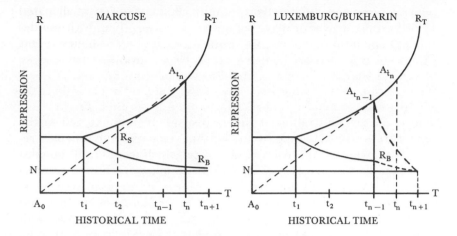

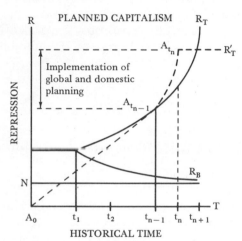

Time key:

N = Realm of Necessity (Ananke)
t_1 = Industrial Revolution
t_n = Theoretical Limit
t_{n-1} = Historical breakdown or transformation point
t_{n+1} = Withering away of the state in a 'true' communist society
A_0t_1 = Traditional precapitalist society
t_1t_2 = Liberal capitalism
t_2t_{n+1} = Advanced capitalism
$t_{n-1}t_{n+1}$ = Planned capitalism *or* movement to 'true' communism
A_tA_0 = Instantaneous apocalypse or descent into barbarism

paths are possible: either a descent into barbarism and the destruction of civilization in an apocalypse (point A_0 at the origin) *or* the supersession of capitalism by a 'true' communist society at t_{n+1}. Should such a supersession indeed occur, there would be a temporary dictatorship of the proletariat. Surplus repression would continue, but at a decreasing rate as the 'withering away of the state' takes place. Eventually, the state would disappear, with communist administration limited to the administration of things instead of men. At that point, surplus repression disappears and all that remains is the unavoidable basic repression of the realm of necessity, which would itself be even more rapidly reduced toward its rock-bottom level with Luxemburg's "triumphant march of the machine" under communist auspices. The state and science would be separated, for the state would no longer exist. Science now would be subordinate to man's needs instead of functioning, as in Brzezinski, as a tool for the domination of man. Surplus repression would be a thing of the past, the 'true' revolution will have at last succeeded, and a humane society will at last have emerged operating at its maximum potential. Actuality and potentiality would be one. This, at any rate, was Luxemburg's vision. But there is an ambiguity in History. The result is not guaranteed, as far as Luxemburg was concerned. It would be contingent on *action,* which would itself run the risk of failure. The descent into barbarism was not to be ruled out as a possibility.

The upper righthand diagram can also be used to describe the dispute between Luxemburg and Nikolai Bukharin. From Bukharin's point of view, Luxemburg's t_{n-1} was too far away for his liking. The supersession of capitalism would come earlier. In Marcusian terms (although Marcuse would hardly subscribe to this use of his concept of repression), the increasing amount of surplus repression would reach its maximum tolerable limit at some point considerably before t_{n-1}. The consciousness of the proletariat, itself an increasing function of an increasing rate of surplus repression, would reach a critical level and, with the disciplined Party Vanguard in full control, the revolution would take place in an outburst of violence establishing the dictatorship of the proletariat. The withering away of the state would then follow, and so on. The difference was more than a dispute over timetables or a matter of revolutionary impatience. Bukharin's point of view became hardened into the *Diamat* of Stalin, with its vulgarization of the Marxian dialectic into a 'scientific' mechanical contraption. History was no longer contingent. The descent into barbarism was ruled out a priori. The end was assured. All of history led inexorably to the triumph of the proletariat. This is the traditional Marxian point of view – with the more intelligent neo-Marxists closer to Luxemburg than to Bukharin, if only because of the absence of any guaranty of success.

An alternate scenario, equally if not more probable, is the historical transformation of capitalism from an unplanned to a *planned* basis, as illustrated in the lower diagram. It is assumed that at t_n capitalism is faced with a finite economic universe where the supply of energy and raw materials is perfectly inelastic. This, of course, is a *theoretical* limit in the same sense that t_n in the upper righthand diagram is Luxemburg's theoretical limit. The political crunch would come well before this economic limit is reached, as post-1973 events seem to portend. Unplanned advanced capitalism would transform itself into a planned system at t_{n-1}, with the total repression curve in the diagram shifting upwards from R_T to R_T'. Again, two possibilities are open: Either planned capitalism in a neomercantilist world will erupt into a series of intense confrontations among capitalist countries competing for access to limited raw materials at each other's expense, and between the capitalist bloc and the LDC bloc (as in Luxemburg's theory of imperialism), leading to the apocalypse in the form of a nuclear war, *or* a forced hegemony will be imposed by the giant superpowers in carving up the world, with total repression (R_T') continuing into the indefinite future at a constant high level. Were R_T' to continue to increase at an increasing rate, in this latter case, we would be back to Marcuse's apocalypse. The assumption is that planned advanced capitalism will succeed in keeping the lid on – which may well prove not to be the case. In the event that it should, global planning will wear the legitimating mask of 'interdependence', and domestic economies will be severely controlled via the political power of cartelized big business fused with a powerful state. In either case, the dream of a utopian solution will remain what it has always been – *a dream based on loving Phantasy and Imagination.*

III

In his theory of social evolution, Habermas does not face up to this last possibilty of a planned, benign authoritarianism or a "technocratic version of Oriental despotism" as the successor of postadvanced capitalism. Marcuse in *One Dimensional Man* sank into a deep despair with the disappearance of the proletariat as *the* historical force of liberation. Habermas, however, keeps the dream of liberation alive by seeking the "Way Out" of capitalist repression through the means of a "communicative ethics." The apocalypse or the descent into barbarism might well be avoided. He rejects all forms of ethical relativism in favor of "justified norms" that are 'true' without being facts *or* values. His critical theory of society is neither empirico-analytical nor normative-analytical. This is Habermas at his most dense. Thomas McCarthy in his "Introduction" to Habermas's *Legitimation Crisis* and Richard J. Bernstein in *The Restructuring of Social and Political Theory* try to unravel Habermas's tortured theory of communicative ethics.

Habermas's purpose is to dissolve through critical theory the legitimating system of advanced technological societies. Just as facts and values and theory and praxis are all inseparable, so are truth and goodness. The unity of truth and goodness, however, can only come about, ideally, in the absence of *all* restraint and *all* forms of domination; that is, in the classless society. In a sense, Habermas is sidestepping the problem of revolutionary praxis and the moral dilemma of dirty hands. In order to achieve that ideal state, the primary function of critical theory, in Habermas, is restricted to the organization of *enlightenment*. Habermas, as Bernstein emphasizes, clearly separates "unconstrained theoretical discourse, enlightenment, and strategic political action." Liberation through enlightenment via reflective knowledge is more reminiscent of Luxemburg's theory of "spontaneity" than it is of Lenin's *What Is to Be Done*, though on the more superficial level of proclaiming: *Laissez eclairer, laissez être intelligent!*

In *Theory and Praxis*, Habermas insisted that the unity of theory and his praxis of enlightenment was *not* a programmatic schema for revolution:

> The organization of action must be distinguished from [the] process of enlightenment. While [critical] theory legitimizes the work of enlightenment . . . it can by no means legitimize *a fortiori* the risky decisions of strategic action. Decisions for the political struggle cannot at the outset be justified theoretically and then be carried out organizationally. . . . *There can be no theory which at the outset can assure a world-historical mission in return for the potential sacrifices.* [3]

Strategic action is certainly "risky" and can therefore never be justified absolutely (we shall return to this theme later), but why a theory must "at the outset" *assure* a world-historical mission is not at all clear. The demand for assurance contradicts the notion of riskiness. At any rate, for Habermas the view that there exists a unity of theory and praxis that can determine unequivocally a plan of action for changing the world presumes a kind of 'scientism' shared by bourgeois theorists and vulgar Marxists. Both claim title to *the* 'true' science that "makes science itself into ideology."

It is not difficult to understand why the writings of Habermas have not appealed to radical, action-oriented groups and why he is dismissed by them as a 'seminar Marxist'.[4] They could easily have quoted Luxemburg in opposition to Habermas (despite the surface similarity of the two in their 'enlightenment' approach to praxis) when she contemptuously dismissed Russian radicals steeped in the belles lettres tradition as:

> [T]he 'subjective method in sociology' which declared *'critical thought'* to be the decisive factor in social development, or which, more precisely, sought to make a down-at-the-heel intelligentsia the agent of historical progress*.[5]

Pas des mains blanches, seulement des mains calleuses! Revolutionary theories are or should be programs for *revolutionary* action; failing that, they are isolated acts of intellectual masturbation, all the more inexcusable when done in public.

Luxemburg was essentially a critic more oriented toward political action than toward theoretical speculation. She was aware of the difficulties in relating ideology to pragmatic action and was perhaps for that reason *anti* systems building. She preferred to maintain the maximum degree of freedom for her revolutionary activities, which meant far more to her than purely theoretical speculation. As her biographer, Peter Nettl, has emphasized, Luxemburg transcended the Marxian framework. Hers was a "moral doctrine which saw in social revolution – and revolutionary activity – not merely the fulfillment of the laws of dialectical materialism but the liberation and progress of humanity."[6] Above all, direct participation in the stream of history, not belle lettrist speculations in the comfort of one's study. But participation was not to be the exclusive domain of a Party Vanguard leading the masses on the basis of some grand, all-encompassing design; it was to be a participation *to lead in order to be led.* She had a great faith in the spontaneity of the proletariat and in their ability to construct their own forms of organization pragmatically on a trial-and-error basis in the *unpredictable* course of the class struggle. Her function as a revolutionary was not to direct the revolution along predetermined lines but to serve it as a midwife does the birth of a child.

Spontaneity was indistinguishable from mass action and her espousal of mass action was not, as it was later vulgarized to be, in opposition to the concept or need for a Party, but rather as a prod to a Party lulled into *in*activity, as was the SPD (*Socialdemokratische Partei Deutschlands*) with its vision of a parliamentary accession to power. Indeed, it

---

*Or, in Marx's words, "professorial socialist riff-raff nonentities in theory and useless in practice."

was her use of the masses and her advocacy of the mass strike as a revolutionary weapon that so enraged the leaders of the SPD, who branded her actions and theories as irresponsible. Her main charge was that the Party had a program of inaction; it had lost its ability to lead and lacked the courage to realize the revolutionary transformation to socialism through mass actions of the proletariat. She was not anti-Party, as simplistic formulations of her spontaneity theory sometimes argue. The Party was a *necessary* ingredient of revolution. Its function, in the words of Nettl, was to serve as "an acceleration chamber in which different elements were fused and their speed of impact heightened."[7] Grand theoretical designs with an èlite, historically retrograde Party Vanguard to implement them under tight control served only to kill the spontaneity of the masses and therefore the "true" liberating revolution itself. Spontaneity was a "long process of national self-enlightenment" involving the proletariat – "that essential harmonic construction without which no Marxist music could be played" (Nettl). The process was as important as the product or, more emphatically, without spontaneity the end product would be deformed into a new tyranny masquerading under the name of socialism. The *humanity* of the revolution would be lost. In this, Luxemburg turned out to be prophetic.

Her basic approach to revolution was *friction* and more friction, leading to the critical mass of class consciousness needed for the true emancipation of mankind. For Luxemburg, the solution "was always more friction, more close engagement; *a confrontation of eye to eye and fist to fist*" with the revolutionary 'élite' serving as a magnet exerting "a powerful field of influence" and not as a "dynamo driving the whole socialist works" from above.[8] But "eye to eye . . . fist to fist" friction implies violence, and violence in turn raises the moral dilemma of dirty hands. Revolution without mud-and-blood is a historical mirage. History, as Maurice Merleau-Ponty has argued, is *Terror*.[9] History is not made in advance – "it depends on the will and audacity of men." Praxis is not a matter of theoretical, *enlightening* knowledge contemplating the world from a distance. Its purpose is to transform it into a better world. To oppose violence is to be counterrevolutionary:

> [T]o abstain from violence toward the violent is to become their accomplice. *We do not have a choice between purity and violence* but between different kinds of violence. . . . Violence is the common origin of all regimes. . . . What matters . . . is not violence but its sense or its future.[10]

The power of capitalism is based on "the power of the few and the resignation of the rest." Marxism, on the other hand, in its unity of theory and *revolutionary* praxis, is a theory of violence that legitimates itself "by the vital need of a humanity already in view."

Habermas's rejection of this particular unity of theory and praxis is a *tamed* Marxism. At bottom, Habermas has not taken us any further than the debate between Luxemburg's concept of revolutionary spontaneity based on escalating friction and Lenin's deadly notion of the Party Vanguard. The problem of *What Is to Be Done?* – from Chernyshevsky to Luxemburg to Lenin – is still with us. Habermas's theory of communicative ethics is a desperate attempt to solve the riddle of getting to utopia without incurring *les mains sales* – socialism through enlightenment! The argument has not advanced much further than where it was, had we been born 100 years ago. One would have to conclude that the transcendence of capitalism to a 'true' socialism is as far away as ever.[11]

Still, Habermas's analysis of capitalist development from its liberal to its advanced stages is far more sophisticated than anything professional economists have done. Indeed, orthodox economists barely pay any attention to the social development of capitalism, and radical economists are, for the most part, still desperately looking for 'internal contradictions' to plant their hopes in, and always finding them in a new form as capitalism moves from one stage to the next, adapting itself conveniently along the way while doing so. And if Luxemburg is right, at least in the idea if not in her theory, that there *is* a limit to capital accumulation and hence to growth, only now for purely exogenous reasons, then perhaps Kissinger is also right in saying that capitalism will adapt to the new problems facing it by moving toward an authoritarian solution – benign or otherwise. And perhaps the 'end' will come via political and economic conflicts, if it comes at all, in a neomercantilist world where the problem of distribution can no longer be made politically irrelevant by limitless growth. We may then be back either in the world of Lukács and Luxemburg where the new circumstance of a finite economic universe, even if only *perceived* to be so contrafactually, will lead to a liberating consciousness of the world proletariat, the resurgence of an *untamed* Marxism, and thus to a *violent* transformation of the world order; or, alternatively, we may find ourselves once more in the world of Jean-Baptiste Colbert and Louis XIV – only this time with enough power to bring the dialectic to an abrupt halt once and for all in another kind of violent transformation. I would not bet on the first.

IV

If this is too bleak a picture, then perhaps Habermas and his followers offer the only remaining hope in identifying praxis not with a specific program for action leading ultimately to a new form of tyranny, but with a process of transforming enlightenment as the only possible way out left to us, no matter how low the probability of its success. But economics and the other social sciences, as we know them today, are hardly moving in this direction. They are still wedded to the scientific project as the only true path to knowledge. They assume the cloak of 'scientific' universality at the price of denying history. They are the 'liberals' of our time guarding the sanctity of the status quo. If the reactionary is concerned with making the past identical with the present and the revolutionary insists on converting the future into the present, the liberal is more concerned with seeing to it "that the present generates another present, not the future." [12]

"The pseudo-objective nature of bourgeois thought," wrote Merleau-Ponty, "the custom of separating problems (economic, political, philosophical, religious, etc.), like the principle of the separation of powers, veils their relation, convergence, and mutual significance in living history"[13] and thus precludes the emergence of the "enlightenment" that Habermas sees as the only role for praxis in exploding the legitimation basis of advanced capitalism. Bourgeois social thought is primarily concerned with developing the implications and definitions of uninterpreted models and the vast accumulation of empirically pretentious data. It denies that the problems of existence can be more effectively met by the union of reason, *passion,* and observation. Impersonal reason and observation have long been the basis of bourgeois theorizing; passion has not, though it colors willy-nilly the observations upon which Reason builds. In the process, bourgeois social thought degenerates into an "intellectual celebration of apathy" and a splintered, fractured empiricism that collapses reasoning into reasonableness. Facts are duly weighed, carefully balanced, and always hedged. "Their power to outrage," as C. Wright Mills argued, "their power to truly *enlighten* in a political way . . . – all that has been blunted and destroyed."[14]

Enlightenment is not the purpose of 'scientific' bourgeois thought. From a Marxian point of view, the purpose of its *wertlos* positivism, its fractured, problem-solving empiricism, is simply to support the status quo and to be the handmaiden of domination and repression. Bourgeois social thought, in other words, has its own ideological commitment and therefore takes on a *political* dimension. Its scientific paradigm, together with the political ideology that supports it, is engaged in the legitimation and consolidation of the existing power structure.

The alternative is to reject the empirico-analytical approach in favor of an "interpretive explication of historically evolving forms of life."[15] Rejecting the "objectivist pretensions" of economists and other social scientists, the *hermeneutic* approach to social analysis places the 'objective' economist within "the boundary of his historical situation." In the words of Albrecht Wellmer:

> In contrast to the positivistic attempt to reduce intentional behavior to observable behavior, that is, to describe social facts as natural facts and, in *this* way, to integrate the social sciences in the "unified science" of empirical analysis . . . the contribution of hermeneutical thought . . . is to be found in its disclosure of the objectivist illusion.[16]

By criticizing the "self-conception of the empirico-analytical social sciences" while allowing them "the partial justification to which they can be shown to be entitled," the hermeneutic approach to social analysis would reject all claims to being a natural science and the illusion of universal laws as a basis for prediction. There is

> no satisfactory and universally valid operationalization of theoretical principles in the social sciences. . . . So much of the specific content of a certain historical period enters into the basic theoretical assumptions . . ., that its hypotheses cannot be transferred without violence to more distant socio-historical situations.[17]

This quotation from Wellmer is identical to what Lukács wrote more than fifty years ago. But hermeneutics goes further in seeking "the connection between explanation and interpretation . . . that is practically and historically oriented." The goal is *explanatory understanding* based on self-understanding and the historical situation. Its concern is to expose, critically, the legitimating forces of society that stand as barriers to liberation, and to make "the development processes which have taken a pathological course *intelligible*." The notion of the 'good life' in a noncoercive society is to stand in opposition to the dominant pseudoscientific forms of self-understanding, which serve only to legitimate *un*freedom by driving it from the realm of consciousness. The hermeneutic approach to social science sees itself "as part of an experimental historical praxis, whose criterion of success is successful emancipation itself." Above all, the critical approach represents the *reentry*, via critical reflection and communication, of the subject back into the objective world; or the subject–object unity that the early Marx talked about and that Lukács and Luxemburg tried to reintroduce into Marxian analysis more than half a century ago.

These may be naive notions; there may be no 'true' revolution possible. The next historical phase may be an advance of advanced capitalism, as has been argued, to a benign form of authoritarianism, or worse; but the fact remains that hermeneutics is the only other intellectual alternative to the positivism of bourgeois social science and vulgar, mechanical Marxism – both of which lead in the end to the same result: *deformed revolutions.* The potential of the 'good' society is still there, and although we may think it will never come, we have no alternative but to think it might – some day.

The point is that the scientific paradigm of bourgeois social theory has ceased to dream and has banished Phantasy and Imagination from the world of 'objective' and 'scientific' truth.[18] For Marcuse,[19] Phantasy and Imagination have a role to play as long as the yawning gap between society's actuality and its potentiality continues to exist. Ideology to Marcuse is a *political,* not a philosophical or sociological, concept. It "considers a doctrine in relation not to the social conditions of its truth or to an absolute truth, but rather to the interest of transformation" – to *political* acts that seek to transform the social structure. Its primary function is to address itself to the realization of human potentialities. Phantasy and Imagination are therefore to be emphasized, as opposed to the facticity of 'scientific' objectivity: "In order to retain what is not yet present as a goal in the present, phantasy is required." Positivism as opposed to Phantasy and Imagination is, in Adorno's words, "the Puritanism of Cognition," with its intolerance for theoretical untidiness and its insistence on abstract formalization divorced from history and from an intractable and tragically misshapen reality. To *impose* order and clarity on a contingent human existence is to ignore the totality for the sake of what can be reduced to manageable quantitative proportions; number pushing, in a word.

Marcuse, Habermas, and other members of the Frankfurt School, whatever their internal differences and whatever the limitation of *their* overall analysis, must at least be credited for trying to do on a broader basis what bourgeois social scientists refuse to do – to 'dream' of a better world, a utopia. Of all the critical theorists, Habermas's analysis of "Late Capitalism" throws new light on the historical transformations of capitalism, even though he ignores the ugly possibilities of its still later transformations and bets on the power of reflexive knowledge alone to find the "Way Out."

IV

The historical world is known only in terms of its past, and the historical process is far too complex, too full of surprises and unexpected developments, to allow any predictions to be made. In each moment of historical time man is faced with a 'field of possibles' radiating out into the future. The field is itself constrained to a *feasible* range by the historical realities of a given point in historical time. Which of these 'feasible' paths will come to pass cannot be known beforehand. A schematic representation would look something like the accompanying diagram.

Historical time is plotted on the horizontal axis and historical 'space' (possible historical configurations for each time period) on the vertical axis. At the time period t_0 only a few paths (solid lines), among the total field of possibles, are open to man, given the concrete conditions serving as a choice-constraint at that time. For example, given the scientific knowledge and technology of 1900, going to the moon in a space rocket was not a 'feasible' possibility. The same is true for each time period from t_0 to t_3. At t_0, for example, the actual path to be taken among the feasible paths cannot be predicted because, as we shall see, of the *contingency* of history. At t_1, looking back, we can determine *after the fact* the path along which we moved from t_0 to t_1. Again, a feasible range of possibles exists at t_1, and so on through t_2 and t_3.

Standing on the pinnacle of the present (t_3) and looking back, the alternate 'possibles' for each past moment of time disappear from view, and the past is not so much postdicted as falsified by an ex post facto imposition of a cause-and-effect relationship raised to the level of 'objective' necessity. All we see is the movement along the zig-zag path of *realized* possibles. Not only is *pre*diction not possible, but even *post*diction fails to appreciate the richness of history in terms of the alternatives foregone, or to profit from them. Historians seldom study the failures of history; they are much too busy elaborating our understanding of past 'successes' and cooking putty into hard-baked clay.

Modern neo-Marxians tell us that for the first time in human history the 'true' social revolution is at last possible – because of the level of technology and its development by capitalism in its trajectory through historical space-time. All revolutions of the past were not only betrayed, they were doomed to fail. But the 'true' revolution today is itself only *one* of many 'possibles', and though feasible for the first time there can be no assurance that it *will* be achieved even though it now can be. Indeed, that has been the main argument of this book.

For Merleau-Ponty, the future is always open and "it is difficult to theorize on a situation in which *historical contingencies* predominate and upset rational forecasts."[20] This is as true for Marxian theory as it is for bourgeois theory. There are no compelling situations in history,

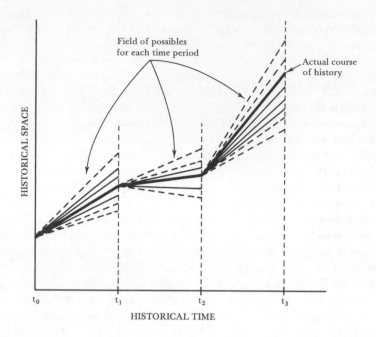

no 'objective' necessities. It is only when a contingent future is concretized in the past that it takes on the appearance of necessity, as does putty when it is transformed into the hard clay of a pot. Man is faced, in other words, with a horizon of possibilities and it is in the face of that horizon that he must make the commitments that, in the aggregate, finally determine the actual path traversed. But in making their commitments, individually or in groups, men *bet* on history and must therefore accept the risk of failure. As Jean-Paul Sartre also argued, "freedom is principally characterized by the fact that you are never sure of winning with it and that the consequences of our acts are probable only. . . . The least little result is attained with difficulty and amidst the greatest uncertainties." Man's fate is to live in a world of "lawless contingencies" and it is "precisely because man is free [that] the triumph of socialism is not at all certain."[21] Sartre was not even willing to rule out a barbarous form of socialism. In the words of Merleau-Ponty:

> History offers us certain factual trends that have to be extrapolated into the future, *but it does not give us the knowledge* with any deductive certainty of which facts are privileged to outline the present to be ushered in. . . . [W]*hatever we do will*

involve risk. . . . [A] decision can lead political man to his death and the revolution into failure.

There is a *spontaneous* movement of objective history, but there is also *human intervention which makes it leap stages* and which cannot be foretold from theoretical schemas.[22]

Man is the actor of history, not a spectator on its sidelines, and the purpose of praxis is to transform the world by action in the *present:* "To live and die for a future projected by *desire* rather than to think and *act* in the present is . . . utopianism."[23] On the question of praxis, Merleau-Ponty is therefore closer to Luxemburg than he is to Habermas.[24] Although history is contingent, it is not "an empty zone in which [to] construct gratuitous projects" of peaceful self-enlightenment. For Merleau-Ponty, all history is based on violence. The question is: violence to what end? In the Marxian context, violence is justified because it "brings reason out of unreason" in the form of a new humanity. But there was a tragic undertone to Merleau-Ponty. [E]*ither one respects the freedom of the proletarians and the revolution is a chimera or else one judges for them what they want and the Revolution becomes Terror"*[25] – which brings us back to Habermas's alternative of socialism through nonviolent enlightenment. The dilemma remains and always will: *les mains blanches* or *les mains sales?*

CODA

Various competing theories, visions, and opinions have been presented. They should be seen only as the various alternatives embodied in a 'field of possibles'. And if, as Merleau-Ponty has argued, the dialectic is open-ended and a priori indeterminate, if there is a contingency in history, an element of unpredictable happenstance, then all visions of a future historical development become futile exercises in self-delusion, no matter how convincing and clever the supporting theory. If so, then that is where the hope lies.

Yet, I expect capitalism to go on . . . and on . . . and on for a long, long time – adapting itself along the way in ways we will not like. And so will intellectual Marxism go on and on adapting its theories in the turbulence of capitalism's wake. *Ainsi soit-il!*

Notes

1. Science, technology, and Marx

1. See especially Herbert Marcuse's pessimistic book, *One Dimensional Man* (Boston, 1964).
2. For excellent summaries of French postwar thought, see Mark Poster, *Existential Marxism in Postwar France: from Sartre to Althusser* (Princeton, N.J., 1975), and David Schalk's analysis of *engagement* versus *embrigadement* in his book *The Spectrum of Political Engagement: Mounier, Benda, Nizan, Brafillach, Sartre* (Princeton, N.J., 1979).
3. Jürgen Habermas, *Toward a Rational Society: Student Protest, Science, and Politics* (Boston, 1970), Chapter 6, "Technology and Science as 'Ideology'"; original German edition, 1968.
4. Jürgen Habermas, *Legitimation Crisis* (Boston, 1975); original German edition, 1973; published under the title *Legitimationsprobleme im Spätkapitalismus* [Problems of Legitimation in Late Capitalism].
5. Habermas, *Legitimation*, p. 82; see also Robert Paul Wolff, "Beyond Tolerance," in Robert Paul Wolff, et al., *A Critique of Pure Tolerance* (Boston, 1965).
6. Ibid., p. 83.
7. William Leiss, *The Domination of Nature* (New York, 1972). Leiss has not been the first to make this observation. See C. S. Lewis, *The Abolition of Man* (New York, 1947): "[W]hat we call Man's power over Nature turns out to be a power exercised by some men over other men with Nature as its instrument."
8. Habermas, *Rational Society*, p. 96; italics supplied.
9. Ibid., pp. 99, 104; italics supplied.
10. Peter Passell and Leonard Ross, *The Retreat from Riches* (New York, 1973).
11. Habermas, *Rational Society*, p. 107; italics supplied.
12. For a critique of Marx's labor theory of value, see Joan Robinson, "The Labor Theory of Value," *Monthly Review* (December 1977).
13. All references to the *Grundrisse: Foundations of the Critique of Political Economy* (which consists of Marx's notebooks and preliminary studies for Volume I of *Capital*) are from the English edition translated by Martin Nicolaus (New York, 1973). A limited two-volume edition was first published in Moscow in 1939 and 1941, of which only three or four copies made their way to the West. The original German edition was not published until 1953. The *Grundrisse* made its first full-version appearance in English translation in 1973.
14. Rosa Luxemburg, *The Accumulation of Capital – an Anti-Critique* (New

115

York, 1972), p. 51; italics supplied. Written in 1915, while she was in prison for her opposition to World War I, and first published posthumously in German in 1921, this book was a reply to the critics of her earlier book, *The Accumulation of Capital* (New York, 1968). The 1972 edition is the first one in English translation.

15. The concept of 'ontology' is a murky point in the literature on Marx. For a discussion of it and the controversies surrounding it, see Herbert Marcuse's 1932 essay, "The Foundations of Historical Materialism,'" in *Studies in Critical Philosophy* (Boston, 1973), pp. 25–8, and Alfred Schmidt, *The Concept of Nature in Marx* (London, 1971), pp. 83–5, 138, 157.

16. Ibid., p. 53.

17. Nikolai Bukharin, *Imperialism and the Accumulation of Capital* (New York, 1972), p. 224; italics supplied; original edition, 1924. This work was written as a critique of Luxemburg's *The Accumulation of Capital;* first translated into English, 1972.

18. Karl Marx, *Theories of Surplus Value* (Moscow, 1968), Part II, n. p. 497; first italics in the original.

2. The limit to capitalist growth

1. For an abbreviated and sensible exposition, see Joan Robinson's "Introduction" to Rosa Luxemburg's *The Accumulation of Capital* (New York, 1968), pp. 13–28, and Kenneth J. Tarbuck's "Editor's Introduction" (especially pp. 16–21) and Appendix I to Rosa Luxemburg's *The Accumulation of Capital – an Anti-Critique* (New York, 1972).

2. Robinson, "Introduction" to Luxemburg, *Accumulation,* p. 13.

3. Bernstein's credentials as a Marxist were impeccable, as he served for a while as Engels's secretary. For an excellent description of the revisionist controversy, see Peter Nettl, *Rosa Luxemburg* (2 vols., London, 1966), Volume 1, Chapter 6, and Peter Gay, *The Dilemma of Democratic Socialism: Eduard Bernstein's Challenge to Marx* (New York, 1952).

4. Michael Tugan-Baranovsky, *Studies on the Theory and History of Commercial Crises in England* (Jena, 1901); quoted in Luxemburg, *Accumulation,* p. 312; italics supplied. The original German edition of Luxemburg's book was published in 1913. The first English translation was in 1951. All references in the text to this work are from the 1968 Modern Reader Paperback edition put out by the Monthly Review Press.

5. Rudolph Hilferding, *Das Finanz Capital* (1910); quoted in Luxemburg, *Anti-Critique,* p. 87; italics supplied.

6. Quoted in Luxemburg, *Accumulation,* p. 315; italics supplied.

7. Luxemburg, *Accumulation,* p. 317; Luxemburg's paraphrase, italics supplied.

8. In her essay, "The Labor Theory of Value" (*Monthly Review,* December 1977), Joan Robinson argues that the labor theory of value "is not something that one can 'believe in' or 'not believe in'. It is a mental construction that may or may not be useful in analyzing reality." As for exploitation, she asks, "Why do we need *value* to show that profits can be made in industry by selling commodities for more than they cost to produce, or to explain the power of those who command finance to push around those who do not?" She goes on to dismiss labor power as

a "metaphor" that explains nothing. In a private communication to the author, she writes that the "labour theory of value has a great aura of ideology but as analysis it is just a definition." Her *Monthly Review* article is also interesting for what she has to say about Marx's confusion between stock and flow concepts and his non sequitur formulation of the falling rate of profit.

9. Luxemburg, *Accumulation*, p. 317.
10. Ibid., p. 320.
11. Ibid., p. 325; italics supplied.
12. Ibid., p. 326.
13. See Nettl, *Luxemburg*, Volume 1, pp. 389–92. Luxemburg had achieved German citizenship by a sham marriage to a German national, Gustav Lübeck, in 1897, just prior to her moving to Berlin in 1898; see Nettl, pp. 109–11.
14. The book was published posthumously in 1925, six years after her murder. It has not yet been translated into English.
15. For a contemporary illustration of this particular Marxian malady, *in extremis*, see Ota Šik, *The Third Way: Marxist-Leninist Theory and Modern Industrial Society* (London, 1976), Part III, Chapter 9.
16. The quotations from Volumes I and II are reproduced on p. 58 of Luxemburg's *Anti-Critique;* italics supplied. All future page references to quotations from the *Anti-Critique* will be given in the text. It would be interesting at this point to note the *full* title of Luxemburg's book, which has not been reproduced in the 1972 English translation: *The Accumulation of Capital, or, What the "Authorities" Have Done with Marxist Theory: an Anti-Critique.* In the original German edition, the word "authorities" appears as *"Epigonen."*
17. See *Anti-Critique*, p. 55. See also Robinson, "Introduction" to Luxemburg, *Accumulation*, pp. 21, 28. As Robinson observes, Luxemburg not only neglected the rise in real wages under capitalism (which the revisionist, Eduard Bernstein, had so strongly argued), she also neglected "the internal inducement to invest provided by technical progress," thus underestimating two important ways in which capitalism could realize its surplus value in a closed system.
18. For a sympathetic critique of Luxemburg's catastrophe theory by Michal Kalecki, see George Feiwel, *The Intellectual Capital of Michal Kalecki* (Knoxville, Tenn., 1975), pp. 55–9. Kalecki agreed with Luxemburg's critique of Marx's expanded reproduction schema as a barren ex post facto equilibrium model, but found that she underestimated the ability of technical progress to sustain capitalist expansion even though it could not, of itself, guaranty the full utilization of productive capacity in the long run (see n. 17 above for a similar comment by Robinson). Moreover, Luxemburg did not fully realize the potential of government expenditures (especially for armaments) to absorb unrealized surplus value through deficit financing. But Kalecki did support Luxemburg's basic position that unlimited expansion at full employment is not a natural state for capitalist society. The fact remains that Luxemburg was one of the first Marxists to pose the problem of effective demand and to anticipate the growth models of Harrod and Domar where the "dual function of investment" leads to an inherent and underlying tendency of productive capacity to outstrip effective

demand in capitalist society. This particular line will be followed up in Chapter 4.

19. It is interesting to compare Luxemburg's theory to Bertil Ohlin's neo-classical theory of interregional and international trade, which ends in a *harmonious* diffusion of capitalism on a worldwide basis with all factor prices equalized and world welfare at its maximum maximorum point.

20. Luxemburg, *Accumulation,* p. 417; italics supplied.

21. Ibid.; italics supplied.

22. Luxemburg's historical sections on imperialism continue to be unsurpassed, particularly her description of the opium trade.

23. The first English edition of Bukharin's *Imperialism* was published by Monthly Review Press along with Luxemburg's *Anti-Critique* in the same volume (also published in English for the first time).

24. This really is the main focus of the dispute, given the stubborn unwillingness of 'orthodox' Marxists to let go of the labor theory of value as a 'scientific' proposition. On the basis of Luxemburg's 'shift' and her groping toward a theory of effective demand, she deserves to go to the head of the class. The development of post–World War I capitalism more than vindicates her shift from 'exploitation' to 'realization'.

25. *Accumulation,* p. 446, italics supplied. On the basis of her theory of imperialism, it is difficult to understand Luxemburg's opposition to World War I and her desperate appeal to the Second International to stop it by coordinating the actions of all socialist parties in the West. (For a possible explanation of Luxemburg's opposition, see Nettl, *Luxemburg,* Volume 2, p. 615). Lenin, on the other hand, rapturously welcomed World War I and was more in line with Marx's own belief, in moments of despair, that the downfall of capitalism would most probably be the result of a capitalist war, his grand theoretical structure notwithstanding. At times Marx, too, rejected the 'long wind' in favor of the 'bated breath' of history [See David McLellan, *Karl Marx: His Life and Thought* (New York, 1973)].

26. Norman Geras, "Barbarism and the Collapse of Capitalism," *New Left Review* (November/December 1973), reprinted as Chapter 1 in *The Legacy of Rosa Luxemburg* (London, 1976).

27. Robinson, in her valuable "Introduction" to Luxemburg's *Accumulation,* points out that "If capitalists from Department II were permitted to lend part of their savings to Department I to be invested as capital, a breakdown would no longer be inevitable" (p. 25). Still, she admits there would be a problem because "there is no guarantee that they will," and this, in Keynesian terms, would mean an insufficiency of effective demand, which was, after all, Luxembug's main point. Robinson therefore suggests converting Luxemburg's "logical necessity" into a "plausible hypothesis." I have no quarrel with this, but the logical *necessity* of Luxemburg is, as she herself pointed out, a *theoretical* limit not likely to be reached in any event. The collapse of capitalism (in thermonuclear wars?) in no way guarantees the supersession of capitalism by socialism as an *historical* necessity. This is by far the more important point. Another, to be elaborated in the last chapter, is that the 'objective' does not exist without reference to the 'subjective', and the link between them is tenuous and full of tension at best. History is contingent and the dialectic is open-ended; descent into apocalyptic

disaster is by no means precluded. Luxemburg would certainly have agreed.

3. The limitless accumulation of capital in postcapitalist society

1. Herbert Marcuse, "The Foundations of Historical Materialism," p. 9, reprinted in his *Studies in Critical Philosophy* (Boston, 1972).
2. *International Herald Tribune,* June 14, 1977.
3. Rosa Luxemburg, *The Accumulation of Capital* (New York, 1968), p. 322. Further page references to this work will be given in the text. In modern terms, Luxemburg ignores the fact that capital is a durable asset spanning more than one production time period. Therefore, the substitution of capital for labor in a capitalist context must take into account the future income to capital over many such periods.
4. Ota Šik, *The Third Way: Marxist-Leninist Theory and Modern Industrial Society* (London, 1976), pp. 114–15; italics supplied.
5. For a detailed description of the debate, see Stephen Rousseas, "The Economic Challenge of Coexistence," *The Correspondent,* (July/August 1963), with comment appended by David Riesman.
6. For an excellent analysis of this problem, based largely on the *Grundrisse,* see Alfred Schmidt, *The Concept of Nature in Marx* (London, 1971); original German edition, 1962. I shall rely heavily on Schmidt's critique and on the lines his book opened up for further research, although he was not specifically concerned with the theory of capital accumulation. Textual references will be to *The Economic and Philosophical Manuscripts of 1844,* Dirk J. Struik, ed. (New York, 1964), and the *Grundrisse: Foundations of the Critique of Political Economy* (New York, 1973).
7. David J. Struik, the editor of the English edition of the *Manuscripts,* points out that the concepts of 'alienation' and 'objectification' can be found in the *Grundrisse* and in Volume III of *Capital* (Ch. 5, Sec. 1). But they represent isolated uses with no supporting analysis behind them. Moreover, Marx was not only opposed to the publication of his early manuscripts, he was also, as Struik shows, against the *reprinting* of those that were. Besides, the works referred to were not published in Marx's lifetime, and the fact remains that the terms scarcely appear in his magnum opus, Volume I of *Capital.* In later life, Marx-the-economist considered himself a scientist and even tried his hand at mathematics – badly as it turned out. See Appendix B to Edmund Wilson's revised edition of *To the Finland Station* (New York, 1972). For a more sympathetic handling, see Hubert C. Kennedy, "Karl Marx and the Foundations of Differential Calculus," *Historia Mathematica,* 4 (1977), pp. 303–18. For Marx's 'scientific' interests in later life, see David McLellan's biography, *Karl Marx: His Life and Thought* (New York, 1973).
8. Quoted in Schmidt, *Nature in Marx,* p. 146.
9. "Foundations," p. 137; italics supplied.
10. For an analysis of this aspect in Marx's later writings, see Schmidt, *Nature in Marx,* Chapter 2:B.
11. Quoted in Schmidt, *Nature in Marx,* p. 135. All direct quotations from Schmidt are taken from Chapters 2 and 4.
12. Quoted in Schmidt, *Nature in Marx,* p. 149.

4. *The problem of capitalist legitimation*

1. See William H. McNeil, *Plagues and Peoples* (New York, 1976), Chapters 1 and 2.
2. Jürgen Habermas, *Legitimation Crisis* (Boston, 1975), p. 21.
3. Georg Lukács, *History and Class Consciousness* (Cambridge, Mass., 1971). All quotations are taken from the first three essays, first published between 1919 and 1921.
4. See Richard J. Bernstein, *The Restructuring of Social and Political Theory* (New York, 1976), p. 173.
5. John Ramsey McCulloch, *The Principles of Political Economy;* quoted by Marx in the *Grundrisse: Foundations of the Critique of Political Economy* (New York, 1973), pp. 615–16; original italics.
6. Habermas, *Legitimation*, p. 28.
7. Ibid., p. 29.
8. Ibid., p. 30.
9. Ibid., p. 36.
10. Cf. Wilhelm Reich, *The Mass Psychology of Fascism* (New York, 1970); original edition, 1942: "With the raising of the standard of living, there was a structural assimilation to the middle class. With the elevation of one's social position, 'one's eyes turned upward'. In times of prosperity this adaptation of middle-class habits was intensified, but the subsequent effect of this adaptation, in times of economic crisis, was to obstruct the full unfolding of revolutionary sentiments" (p. 72).
11. Habermas, *Legitimation*, p. 47; italics supplied. Habermas tends to underestimate the resiliency of capitalism and its ability to adapt to a sudden exogenously induced structural change in the system. This matter is left to Chapter 5.
12. Ibid., p. 51.
13. Habermas also bases a part of his argument concerning the 'internal contradictions' of advanced capitalism on James O'Connor's *The Fiscal Crisis of the State* (New York, 1973). This is unfortunate, for O'Connor has mistaken the very strength of capitalism for its weakness. The co-optation ability of capitalism is not easily compromised, especially when its system of legitimation is at stake. O'Connor's theory would have some force if capitalism were in a state of *permanent* crisis – which Marx himself denied.
14. Habermas, *Legitimation*, p. 62. This is a highly exaggerated and incorrect appraisal of advanced capitalism, as will be argued later in this and the next chapter. It is a product of the Marxian obsession with 'internal contradictions', usually within the context of a mechanical dialectic. It is also part and parcel of Habermas's "systems analysis" approach to advanced capitalism.
15. See Evsey Domar, "Expansion and Employment," *American Economic Review* (March 1947), pp. 34–55; reprinted in *Essays in the Theory of Economic Growth* (New York, 1957), pp. 83–108. The implicit assumptions of this model are that the state of technology is fixed and that once aggregate investment decisions have been made, the ability to substitute capital for labor no longer exists, i.e., the production function is made of hard-baked clay, not putty. The neoclassical introduction of technological change and capital–labor substitutability, no mat-

ter how contrived, serves only to mitigate the basic problem without quite doing away with it.
16. Ibid., pp. 98–9; italics supplied.
17. Michal Kalecki, "Political Aspects of Full Employment," *The Political Quarterly,* Volume XIV, Number 4 (October/December 1943), pp. 322–31.
18. Although Kalecki wrote his article in 1943, the main line of his argument saw its ultimate justification in 1977. Carter ran for the presidency in the post-Vietnam depression of 1976, as Kennedy ran in 1960 in the aftermath of the Korean War, with a pledge to restore full employment through appropriate fiscal and monetary measures. It was the old Kennedy refrain of "Let's get America moving again." When Carter assumed the presidency, unemployment as officially measured was close to 8 percent of the civilian labor force. His promise was to reduce it to 6.5 percent (!) by the end of his first term and to about 6 percent by the end of 1984. On April 14, 1977, he announced the withdrawal of his proposed $10 billion (American billion) tax rebate to consumers and the cancellation of the proposed increase in the tax credit to businessmen for new investment. The grounds for his reversal were that the economy was on an upswing and that inflationary pressures would be aggravated by the tax cuts. To maintain a 'sound dollar', deficit financing would have to be trimmed. The following day, according to the *New York Times,* "The nation's financial markets gave President Carter a resounding vote of approval. . . . Stock prices rose sharply in the heaviest trading of the year," and in the opinion of a Chase Manhattan Bank economist, President Carter's decision put the government budget in a "sounder fiscal position." "Led by Arthur Burns, the Chairman of the Federal Reserve," observed the *Times* in an editorial, "conservatives argued that . . . the risk of added inflation . . . was *too high a price to pay for at best, a moderate reduction in unemployment*" (Italics supplied).
19. John Maynard Keynes, *The General Theory of Employment, Interest and Money* (New York, 1936), p. 254; italics supplied.
20. See George Feiwel, *The Intellectual Capital of Michal Kalecki* (Knoxville, Tenn., 1975), pp. 55–8.
21. Kalecki, "The Fascism of Our Times," in *The Last Phase in the Transformation of Capitalism* (New York, 1972), p. 100; italics supplied.
22. It is true that World War II gave rise to radar, atomic power, jet engines, and miniaturized computer circuitry, but modern weapons systems are so highly specialized that spinoff effects to the civilian sector are relatively small. Even if lasers and satellite communications are possible contemporary spinoffs, the alternative costs of military research and development in terms of discoveries foregone by the skewing of scientific research cannot be dismissed out of hand, though of course they cannot be measured.
23. Ruth Leger Sivard, *World Military and Social Expenditures,* WMSE (World Military and Social Expenditures) Reports (Leesburg, Va., 1974 and 1976). Sivard pioneered research in this area under the U.S. Arms Control and Disarmament Agency (ACDA) from 1965 until 1972 when, under the Nixon administration, the ACDA discontinued its annual reports. She has continued her work for the Institute for World

Order. I have borrowed heavily from Sivard's work and the statistical tables published as appendices to her reports.

24. For some black humor that systematized this insanity in governmental jargon, see Leonard C. Lewin, *Report from Iron Mountain on the Possibility of Peace* (New York, 1967). When the book first came out, supposedly as a secret government document leaked to Lewin, it was taken seriously by virtually all reviewers. Its main point was that war was the basic social system and the underlying structural force of society. War, it was argued, promoted social cohesion and nuclear war would itself reverse the genetic effects of old-fashioned war and even *improve* the species by offsetting the regressive effects of medical progress. To do away with war without substituting something else in its place, equally as wasteful and threatening, would bring society down. Peace was an unacceptable substitute for war. An arms race in a Cold War context would do nicely. The willful pollution of the environment would do as well. Speculation had it that John Kenneth Galbraith was the secret author. That Lewin's spoof was taken seriously is a measure of the degree to which insanity had become institutionalized into a mad rationality that carried conviction.

25. The argument can even be applied to new equipment in some cases. In 1977, a controversy broke out over selling seven very advanced AWACs (Airborne Warning and Control Systems) to Iran at a total purchase price of $1.2 billion (American billion). Commented the *Washington Post* in an editorial (July 28, 1977): "[T]here is a strong Pentagon pressure to recapture by exports some of the huge development costs ($2.8 billion). NATO is gagging on the price. Hence the drive to sell to Iran."

26. See Chapter 3, no. 5.

5. Beyond advanced unplanned capitalism

1. By far the best account of mercantilism is to be found in the revised two-volume study of Eli F. Heckscher, *Mercantilism*, 2d ed. (London, 1955). The original Swedish edition was published in 1931, the English edition in 1935.

2. "Maintaining the Momentum Toward Peace," Bureau of Public Affairs, U.S. State Department, Office of Media Services, September 23, 1974; italics supplied.

3. Leo Strauss, *On Tyranny* (Ithaca, N.Y., 1963), pp. 22, 26; italics supplied.

4. Zbigniew Brzezinski, "America in the Technetronic Age," *Encounter* (January 1968), and *Between Two Ages: America's Role in the Technetronic Age* (New York, 1970).

5. *Report of the National Advisory Commission on Civil Disorders* (New York, 1968). See the series of articles titled "Two Societies: America Since the Kerner Report," *New York Times*, February 26, 27, 28, and March 1, 1978.

6. *San Diego Union*, August 25, 1974; cited in a special MIT study for the U.S. State Department, Special Report No. 17, July 1975.

7. All the Kissinger quotations are taken from U.S. State Department reprints of his speeches around the country and his frequent testimony before congressional committees; italics supplied.

8. As the then new secretary of state, Cyrus Vance acknowledged, in his testimony before the U.S. House Ad Hoc Committee on Energy (May 4, 1977), the OPEC countries "have acquired wealth, power and influence in a brief period." But, he added, "They are becoming integrated step-by-step into the world economic and financial systems" – of the capitalist bloc, of course. On July 25, 1977, *Pravda* expressed the Soviet Union's concern over OPEC's co-optation by the West. It warned OPEC that the capitalist "imperialists" controlled the "transportation, processing and distribution" of oil as evidenced by the fact that "the OPEC countries now account for more than 90 percent of the export of oil in the capitalist world while holding only 2 percent of the tanker fleet." It urged OPEC to acquire its own fleet of oil tankers to offset their dependence on the capitalist bloc (*New York Times*, July 26, 1977).

9. The Carter administration's use of "human rights" struck some observers as a calculated undermining of East–West détente, along with its posture in the SALT (Strategic Arms Limitation Talks) negotiations. The State Department hired the Center for International Studies of MIT to do a special study on 'interdependence'. In reviewing possible policy alternatives, the MIT report, though rejecting the option, observed that "a purely cynical U.S. strategy might even re-escalate the Cold War in order to bring its allies back into economic line." This would be tantamount to selling 'security futures' analogous to practices in the commodity market. (See U.S. State Department, *Special Report No. 17*, July 1975, p. 20, for the "cynical" alternative). Indeed, Carter's "human rights" campaign is referred to in European capitals as "Carter's Little Cold War."

10. In starker terms, Sir Neil Cameron, Britain's Chief of Defense Staff, warned NATO that in the near future it might "be obliged to wage peripheral wars to keep its share of world resources." *International Herald Tribune*, July 18, 1977; summary of a *Newsweek* interview with France's president, Valery Giscard d'Estaing.

11. For Kissinger's speech and the final United Nations report, see "Results of the Seventh Special Session of the U.N. General Assembly: September 1–16, 1975," U.S. State Department, *Selected Documents No. 2*. For an excellent and critical analysis of the special session, see especially Geoffrey Barraclough, "The Haves and the Have Nots," *New York Review of Books*, May 13, 1976, and his earlier article, "Wealth and Power: the Politics of Food and Oil," *New York Review of Books*, August 7, 1975.

12. MIT–State Department Study (No. 17, July 1975); italics supplied.

13. On July 22, 1977, the United States began its stockpiling of Arabian light, the best Saudi Arabian crude oil, in Louisiana by pumping 412,000 barrels into a salt dome. The goal is to reach an oil reserve of a billion (American billion) barrels. Some of the salt domes are one-and-a-half miles across and up to 50,000 feet deep, and are capable of holding 61 million barrels of oil (*New York Times*, July 23, 1977).

14. *New York Times*, April 19, 1976; italics supplied.

15. The debate has been reproduced in *Challenge Magazine* (March/April 1976).

16. Robert Heilbroner, "The American Plan: National Economic Planning Will Arrive When Businessmen Demand It – and Demand It They

Will, to Save the Capitalist System," *New York Times Magazine* (January 25, 1976).

17. See Jeff Frieden, "The Trilateral Commission: Economics and Politics in the 1970s," *Monthly Review* (December 1977), and Richard Falk, "A New Paradigm for International Legal Studies" *Yale Law Journal* (April 1975). See also, "Recent Developments in French Planning: Some Lessons for the United States," U.S. House and Senate Joint Economic Committee, Subcommittee on Economic Growth and Stabilization (December 16, 1977).

18. See William L. Shirer, *The Collapse of the Third Republic: an Inquiry into the Fall of France in 1940* (New York, 1969), and Robert Paxton, *Vichy France* (New York, 1972).

19. See Chapter 2 for the charges hurled against Rosa Luxemburg by her critics – namely, that in her theory the working classes of the capitalist countries would become passive, and in the event of a Third World revolt would support the capitalist class in suppressing it.

6. Beyond capitalism?

1. Herbert Marcuse, *Eros and Civilization* (New York, 1961); original edition, 1955.

2. Herbert Marcuse, *One Dimensional Man* (Boston, 1967), p. 231; italics supplied.

3. (Boston, 1973); original edition, 1971. The quotation is taken from Richard J. Bernstein, *The Restructuring of Social and Political Theory* (New York, 1976), p. 217; italics supplied.

4. See the *New York Times*, April 3, 1977, on Klaus-Uwe Benneter, a young radical lawyer in the Marxist wing of the SPD (claiming 350,000 members under the age of 35). They are action-oriented and willing to cooperate with the Italian and French Eurocommunists. They have a program for action that, apart from Habermas's enlightenment function, calls for fundamental economic change. Benneter is quoted as saying that the Young Socialists "have been lacking in perspective and haven't pointed the way to the future."

5. Rosa Luxemburg, *The Accumulation of Capital* (New York, 1968), p. 274; italics supplied. The footnoted quotation from Marx is in Yvonne Kapp, *Eleanor Marx* (Vol. I, New York, 1977), p. 208.

6. Peter Nettl, *Rosa Luxemburg* (2 vols., London, 1966), Volume 1, p. 12. Nettl's analysis of Luxemburg's theory of spontaneity is by far the best and the most insightful available. It serves as a good antidote to its simplistic popularization in the West and its assassination at the hands of Russian Marxists.

7. Ibid., Volume 2, p. 509.

8. Ibid., Volume 1, p. 291; italics supplied.

9. Maurice Merleau-Ponty, *Humanism and Terror* (Boston, 1969); original French edition, 1947.

10. Ibid., p. 109; italics supplied.

11. The recent emergence of the *nouveaux philosophes* in France and the debate they have provoked is an interesting phenomenon in this connection. See Jacques Julliard, "La Gauche et ses intellectuels," in *Le Nouvel Observateur*, June 6, 1977; Claude Roy, "Les disc jockeys de la

pensée," *Le Nouvel Observateur*, July 18, 1977; "Notes and Commentary," *Telos*, No. 33, (Fall 1977); and Cornelius Castoriadis, "The French Left, *Telos*, No. 34, (Winter 1977–8).

12. Jean-Paul Sartre, "Materialism and Revolution," in William Barrett and Henry D. Aiken, eds., *Philosophy in the Twentieth Century*, Volume 3 (New York, 1962), p. 348.
13. Merleau-Ponty, *Terror*, p. 124.
14. C. Wright Mills, "Letter to the New Left," *New Left Review* (September/October 1960); italics supplied.
15. Albrecht Wellmer, *Critical Theory of Society* (New York, 1974), p. 32.
16. Ibid., p. 34.
17. Ibid., pp. 35–6.
18. For a provocative argument along these lines from an anarchist point of view, see Paul Fayerabend, *Against Method* (London, 1975).
19. Herbert Marcuse, "Philosophy and Critical Theory," in *Negations: Essays in Critical Theory* (Boston, 1968).
20. Merleau-Ponty, *Terror*, p. 137; italics supplied.
21. Sartre, "Revolution," p. 346.
22. Merleau-Ponty, *Terror*, pp. 65, 89, 93; italics supplied.
23. Ibid., p. 8; italics supplied.
24. Yet, toward the end of his life in 1961, Merleau-Ponty became a disillusioned man withdrawn from the world of political action. A decade later his former collaborator, Jean-Paul Sartre, was handing out Maoist tracts on the streets of the *Quartier Latin* defying arrest. In this connection, the tragedy of Sartre lay in his own importance.
25. Merleau-Ponty, *Terror*, p. 117.

Selected bibliography

Bernstein, Richard J., *The Restructuring of Social and Political Theory* (New York, 1976).
Brzezinski, Zbigniew, *Between Two Ages: America's Role in the Technetronic Age* (New York, 1970).
Bukharin, Nikolai, *Imperialism and the Accumulation of Capital* (New York, 1972).
Chaliand, Gérard, *Revolution in the Third World* (New York, 1977).
Domar, Evsey, *Essays in the Theory of Economic Growth* (New York, 1957)
Fayerabend, Paul, *Against Method* (London, 1975).
Feiwel, George, *The Intellectual Capital of Michal Kalecki* (Knoxville, Tenn., 1975).
Gay, Peter, *The Dilemma of Democratic Socialism: Eduard Bernstein's Challenge to Marx* (New York, 1952).
Geras, Norman, *The Legacy of Rosa Luxemburg* (London, 1976).
Habermas, Jürgen, *Legitimation Crisis* (Boston, 1975).
  Toward a Rational Society: Student Protest, Science and Politics (Boston, 1970).
Heckscher, Eli F., *Mercantilism*, 2d ed. (2 vols., London, 1955).
Kalecki, Michal, *The Last Phase in the Transformation of Capitalism* (New York, 1972).
Kapp, Yvonne, *Eleanor Marx* (2 vols., New York, 1977).
Leiss, William, *The Domination of Nature* (New York, 1972).
  The Limits to Satisfaction: an Essay on the Problem of Needs and Commodities (Toronto, 1976).
Lewin, Leonard C., *Report from Iron Mountain on the Possibility of Peace* (New York, 1967).
Lukács, Georg, *History and Class Consciousness* (Cambridge, Mass., 1971).
Luxemburg, Rosa, *The Accumulation of Capital* (New York, 1968).
  The Accumulation of Capital – an Anti-Critique (New York, 1972).
Marcuse, Herbert, *Eros and Civilization* (New York, 1961).
  Negations: Essays in Critical Theory (Boston, 1968).
  One Dimensional Man (Boston, 1974).
  Studies in Critical Philosophy (Boston, 1973).
Marx, Karl, *Capital,* Kerr Edition (3 vols., Chicago, 1905).
  The Economic and Philosophical Manuscripts, Dirk J. Struik, ed. (New York, 1964).
  Grundrisse: Introduction to the Critique of Political Economy, trans. Martin Nicolaus (New York, 1973).
  Theories of Surplus Value (Moscow, 1968).
McLellan, David, *Karl Marx: His Life and Thought* (New York, 1973).

Selected bibliography

Merleau-Ponty, Maurice, *Humanism and Terror* (Boston, 1969).
Nettl, Peter, *Rosa Luxemburg* (2 vols., London, 1966).
Paxton, Robert, *Vichy France* (New York, 1972).
Poster, Marc, *Existential Marxism in Postwar France: from Sartre to Althusser* (Princeton, N.J., 1975).
Reich, Wilhelm, *The Mass Psychology of Fascism* (New York, 1970).
Report of the National Advisory Commission on Civil Disorders (New York, 1968).
Sampson, Anthony, *The Arms Bazaar: from Lebanon to Lockheed* (New York, 1977).
Sartre, Jean-Paul, *Between Existentialism and Marxism* (New York, 1974).
    Critique of Dialectical Reason (London, 1977).
Schmidt, Alfred, *The Concept of Nature in Marx* (London, 1971).
Shirer, William L., *The Collapse of the Third Republic: an Inquiry into the Fall of France in 1940* (New York, 1969).
Sivard, Ruth Leger, *World Military and Social Expenditures* (Leesburg, Va., 1974, 1976).
Strauss, Leo, *On Tyranny* (Ithaca, N.Y., 1963).
Wellmer, Albrecht, *Critical Theory of Society* (New York, 1974).
Wilson, Edmund, *To the Finland Station,* rev. ed. (New York, 1972).
Wolff, Robert Paul, et al., *A Critique of Pure Tolerance* (Boston, 1965).
Workshop on Alternative Energy Strategies (WAES), *Energy: Global Prospects, 1985–2000* (New York, 1977).

Index